As Resplendent As Rubies

The Mother's Blessing and God's Favour towards Women II

As Resplendent As Rubies:
The Mother's Blessing & God's Favour Towards Women II

© Anne Hamilton and Natalie Tensen 2020

Published by Armour Books
P. O. Box 492, Corinda QLD 4075 Australia

Cover Image: © Hakase | istockphoto
Interior Design and Typeset by Book Whispers

ISBN: 978-1-925380-20-0

A catalogue record for this book is available from the National Library of Australia

All rights reserved. No part of this publication may be reproduced, stored in, or introduced into a retrieval system, or transmitted, in any form, or by any means (electronic, mechanical, photocopying, recording or otherwise) without the prior written permission of the publisher.

Please note: the spelling, grammar and punctuation in this book are consistent with Australian language conventions.

As Resplendent As Rubies

The Mother's Blessing and God's Favour towards Women II

Anne Hamilton
Natalie Tensen

With prayers by
Dell Hamilton & Natalie Tensen

With preface by
Milly Bennitt Young

Scripture quotations marked BSB are taken from the The Holy Bible, Berean Study Bible, BSB Copyright ©2016 by Bible Hub Used by Permission. All Rights Reserved Worldwide.

Scripture quotations marked ESV are taken from the ESV® Bible (The Holy Bible, English Standard Version®), copyright © 2001 by Crossway, a publishing ministry of Good News Publishers. Used by permission. All rights reserved

Scripture quotations marked ISV are taken from the Holy Bible: International Standard Version®. Copyright © 1996-forever by The ISV Foundation. ALL RIGHTS RESERVED INTERNATIONALLY. Used by permission.

Scripture quotations marked KJV are taken from the King James Version of the Bible. Public domain.

Scripture quotations marked NAS are taken from the New American Standard Bible®, Copyright © 1960, 1962, 1963, 1968, 1971, 1972, 1973, 1975, 1977, 1995 by The Lockman Foundation. Used by permission. (www.Lockman.org)

Scripture quotations marked NLT are taken from the Holy Bible, New Living Translation, copyright 1996, 2004. Used by permission of Tyndale House Publishers, Inc., Wheaton, Illinois 60189. All rights reserved.

Scripture quotations marked NIV are taken from the Holy Bible, New International Version®, NIV®. Copyright © 1973, 1978, 1984, 2011 by Biblica, Inc.™ Used by permission of Zondervan. All rights reserved worldwide. www.zondervan.com The "NIV" and "New International Version" are trademarks registered in the United States Patent and Trademark Office by Biblica, Inc.™.

Scripture quotations marked NKJV are taken from the New King James Version. Copyright © 1982 by Thomas Nelson, Inc. Used by permission. All rights reserved.

Scripture quotations marked WEB are taken from the World English Bible, a modernisation of the American Standard Version (ASV). Public domain.

Also in this series

As Resplendent as Rubies with Study Guide
The Mother's Blessing & God's Favour Towards Women II

More Precious than Pearls:
The Mother's Blessing & God's Favour Towards Women

More Precious than Pearls with Study Guide
The Mother's Blessing & God's Favour Towards Women

Jesus and the Healing of History

\# 1 ***Like Wildflowers, Suddenly***
\# 2 ***Bent World, Bright Wings***
\# 3 ***Silk Shadow, Rings of Gold***

Art and Photo Credits

Cover © Hakase | istockphoto

Page 5 © Tomert | Dreamstime.com

Page 21 © Andrzej Burzek | istockphoto

Page 37 © Yuganov Konstantin | istockphoto

Page 53 © ipopba | istockphoto

Page 63 © Kevin Carden | lightstock

Page 77 © Kevin Carden | lightstock

Page 89 © Forgiven Photography, Travis Silva | lightstock

Pages x and 102 © Tracey White, facebook.com/artisttraceywhite

Contents

1	Woman and Mother: Kingmaker	6
2	Woman and Mother: Visionary	22
3	Woman and Mother: Navigator	38
4	Woman and Mother: Sentinel	54
5	Woman and Mother: Mentor and Coach	64
6	Woman: Culture-changer	78
7	Woman and Mother: Princess	90
	Endnotes	103

Preface

FROM THE BEGINNING, GOD GAVE men and women different functions that complement each other. The first woman and pattern that we follow was called 'Chava' in Hebrew. In English she is known as 'Eve', *the life-giver.*

Giving life is uniquely woven into our design. This can flow through our words and actions as we walk intimately with Jesus and assimilate His character and nature.

'In Him was life, and that life was the light of men.' John 1:4 BSB

The manner in which we are called to bear His expression of life is unique to each of us. We may not be called to sit on the front row of church as the pastor's wife. Clapping politely for him. Reading the notices in a sweet voice and calling in volunteers for children's church.

But we are called to sit at Jesus' feet, just like Mary.

'Mary has chosen the good portion, and it will not be taken away from her.' Luke 10:42 BSB

What we receive as we sit with Him is ours forever.

We can still be feminine, yet war like Deborah in prayer or break out in extravagant worship like Miriam.

As women chosen and honoured by Jesus, may we find joy in who He made us to be so that we can shine in whatever capacity He has called us.

As women we are privileged to receive and incubate the timeless seed of His Word. That is His whisper. To nurture this seed through to completion. Bringing forth life and the perfection of His desire for us.

Be blessed as you read this jewel of a book.

Milly Bennitt Young
Tennessee, USA

Introduction

ONE OF THE SURPRISING ASPECTS of the Scriptural record is its recognition of women as pioneers and trailblazers. For as long as we can remember, biblical women have been sidelined into a secondary role. To rip the veil off that particular cultural mindset and to see the level of honour women are actually accorded in the Bible has not been easy—but it has been delightful, thrilling and affirming.

It's been a real eye-opener to discover that the Bible itself portrays women as visionaries and kingmakers, cupbearers and watchmen, mentors and benefactors, bridge-builders, navigators and—of all mysterious things—God-namers!

In the first book in this series, we looked at the stories of the Exodus. There we uncovered a little-known theme: the heroic stand of women who remained faithful to God while men repeatedly chose idolatry. Perhaps 'little-known' is not quite the right description. After all, rabbinic commentators frequently acknowledge the role of the 'mothers of Israel' during this time. Still it's true to say that, outside these circles, the significance of the women in Scripture and their contributions are rarely recognised for what they are.

We invite you to join us in adventuring back into the Bible for this second volume on women and mothers. Open yourself to the loveliness of God's quiet favour towards women—it's an overflowing treasury of grace and blessing very often hidden in plain sight!

Anne Hamilton
Natalie Tensen
Queensland, Australia

1
Woman and Mother: Kingmaker

1
Woman and Mother: Kingmaker

IN AUSTRALIA BACK IN 2015, McDonald's launched an extremely unusual ad campaign. It was so out of character for the brand that some people actually dubbed it 'Un McDonald's.' For a start, the background music had an unmissable classical air. The ad featured the powerful and rousing anthem, *Zadok the Priest*, originally composed by Handel for the coronation of George II almost three centuries ago.

I was always vaguely disappointed a full orchestra and massed choir didn't suddenly appear under the golden arches with Ronald McDonald conducting. It would have been amazing to hear them belt out the lyrics:

> *Zadok the priest, and Nathan the prophet anointed Solomon king.*
>
> *And all the people rejoiced, rejoiced, rejoiced*
> *And all the people rejoiced, rejoiced, rejoiced*
> *Rejoiced, rejoiced, rejoiced*
> *And all the people rejoiced, rejoiced,*
> *rejoiced and said:*
>
> *God save the king*

Long live the king
God save the king
May the king live forever
Amen, amen, alleluia, alleluia, amen, amen
Amen, amen, alleluia, amen.[1]

Now these words obviously aren't an exact quote from Scripture. They are a paraphrase of the coronation scene in the first chapter of 1 Kings and are based on the Authorised Version of verses 38–39:

> **So Zadok the priest, and Nathan the prophet**, *and Benaiah the son of Jehoiada, and the Cherethites, and the Pelethites, went down, and caused Solomon to ride upon king David's mule, and brought him to Gihon.*
>
> *And Zadok the priest took a horn of oil out of the tabernacle, and* **anointed Solomon**. *And they blew the trumpet; and all the people said, God save King Solomon.*
>
> **And all the people** *came up after him, and the people piped with pipes, and* **rejoiced with great joy**, *so that the earth rent with the sound of them.*

1 Kings 1:38–39 KJV

The words I've emphasised in bold are the main basis of Handel's lyrics, and we learn several things from this description.

First: it's obviously the role of a priest and a prophet to anoint a king

Second: to anoint the king, the priest used a horn of oil

Third: the son of David rode a donkey to his coronation

Fourth: he was taken to Gihon, a spring of water

Fifth: the people rejoiced greatly

Sixth: the people called out, 'God save…'

Now, in fact, when it comes to that last point, the King James Version has taken a tiny bit of liberty. The actual Hebrew is closer to 'Long live King Solomon' than 'God save King Solomon!' Handel was more correct in his lyrics than the translators of the Authorised Version were in their words.

But, to give them their due, the translators took this licence for a very good theological reason. They clearly wanted to ensure the maximum number of parallels between this account of a son of David riding a donkey through Jerusalem with that of 'great David's greater Son' riding into Jerusalem a thousand years later.

> *They brought the donkey and the colt and laid their cloaks on them, and Jesus sat on them.*
>
> *A massive crowd spread their cloaks on the road, while others cut branches from the trees and spread them on the road. The crowds that went ahead of Him and those that followed were shouting: 'Hosanna to the Son of David!'*
>
> *'Blessed is He who comes in the name of the Lord!'*
>
> *'Hosanna in the highest!'*
>
> Matthew 21:7–9 BSB

Yes, when Jesus rode into Jerusalem and palm branches were spread out on the ground before Him, He was effectively coming as the Son of David to His coronation. And the cries of Hosanna meant *Please save us!*

The King James translators didn't want us to miss the fact the coronation of Solomon, the son of David, foreshadowed the triumphal entry to Jerusalem by Jesus, the Son of David.

So let's tick off the aspects of coronation involved.

Son of David, tick.

Riding a donkey, tick.

Through Jerusalem, tick.

People rejoicing greatly, tick.

People wanting to be saved, tick.

But wait. When was He anointed? When was He washed? Who performed the kingmaker[2] functions? Where were the oil and the spring of water?

It's not as if we can shrug our shoulders and say it doesn't really matter. It does. In ancient times, both anointing oil and 'living water' were absolutely essential ritual elements in a royal coronation.

So did Jesus miss out?

Well, to discover the answer to that, let's back up twelve hours or so and look at the events of the previous evening. Now, to us, that's the day before—but to the Hebrew people, for whom a calendar date officially started as the sun set over the western horizon, it was still part of the same day.

Jesus had been invited to dinner in His honour in the village of Bethany about three kilometres from Jerusalem. We learn the timing from John's account of events. He informs us it was 'six days before the Passover' and he also tells us that Lazarus, Martha and Mary were at the dinner.

Luke adds another detail: the host was a Pharisee named Simon. Both Matthew and Mark give us additional information: Simon had leprosy.

These four different testimonies with slightly different details have led some Bible commentators to think that a very similar incident happened twice during the time of Jesus' ministry. I don't think it's necessary to draw that conclusion: only John sets the dinner in a very specific timeframe.

John also is the only one to tell us that it was Mary who anointed Jesus' feet and that it was Judas who complained about the extravagance.

Matthew agrees that the event happened in Bethany, and he places it in the last week of Jesus' life.[3] He doesn't mention any feet being anointed but tells us about the head; nor does he identify Judas as the culprit when it comes to complaints about the woman's wastefulness—he pins it on *all* the disciples.

Mark is bit more coy. He concurs with Matthew that, yes, it was Bethany, yes, it was Simon the Leper, and yes, Jesus was anointed on the head—but it was 'those present' who did the complaining. Vague, general and definitely not pointing any fingers at any disciples. But he is the one who mentions that the woman was given a tough time and told off harshly by the indignant guests.

As I said, I don't think we need two different incidents to account for the different details—I think, like any witnesses recounting their version of events, the gospel writers emphasised what was important to them. We can build up a fuller, more rounded picture from their different perspective on the events.[4] So let's look closely at Luke's account because it's the most detailed:

> *A woman in that town who lived a sinful life learned that Jesus was eating at the Pharisee's house, so she came there with an alabaster jar of perfume. As she stood behind him at his feet weeping, she began to wet his feet with her tears.[5] Then she wiped them with her hair, kissed them and poured perfume on them.*
>
> *When the Pharisee who had invited him saw this, he said to himself, 'If this man were a prophet, he would know who is touching him and what kind of woman she is—that she is a sinner.'*

> *Jesus answered him, 'Simon, I have something to tell you.'*
>
> *'Tell me, teacher,' he said.*
>
> *'Two people owed money to a certain moneylender. One owed him five hundred denarii, and the other fifty. Neither of them had the money to pay him back, so he forgave the debts of both. Now which of them will love him more?*
>
> *Simon replied, 'I suppose the one who had the bigger debt forgiven.'*
>
> *'You have judged correctly,' Jesus said.*
>
> *Then he turned toward the woman and said to Simon, 'Do you see this woman? I came into your house. You did not give me any water for my feet, but she wet my feet with her tears and wiped them with her hair. You did not give me a kiss, but this woman, from the time I entered, has not stopped kissing my feet. You did not put oil on my head, but she has poured perfume on my feet. Therefore, I tell you, her many sins have been forgiven—as her great love has shown. But whoever has been forgiven little loves little.'*

Luke 7:37–47 NIV

Bear in mind that this is the evening before Jesus rides, as the Son of David, on a donkey into Jerusalem. Who anointed Him with oil? Who washed Him with living water?

Every writer testifies that it was a woman. There is no dispute about that.

Simon had his opportunity to be the kingmaker—to take the role foreshadowed by Zadok the priest and Nathan the prophet—but he let it slip by.[6]

Not only was it a woman, but a sinful one at that.

Jesus didn't just lift her up, He reminded her that her past did not define her. He effectively appointed her to the office of kingmaker. After all, He could have asked one of the disciples to fulfil that role or even to ratify her action by repeating the anointing and washing. But He didn't. He simply let it stand.

And if we are tempted to think to ourselves that Mary fell into this position by default, we can disabuse ourselves of that notion fairly quickly. You see, she wasn't the only kingmaker in the life of Jesus. There were others.

To redeem the world, Jesus needed to be proclaimed its king—in order that He could represent the whole of humanity. In theory, all that would be needed would be to find someone with the authority to say so. But of course, the world is a complex, fragmented place and it certainly wasn't ever going to be as simple as finding a single someone who could declare that was the case.

Now let's note that the ancient rabbinical world was divided three ways: Judea, Samaria, the rest of the world. In other words, to be proclaimed 'King of the World', Jesus had to be heralded as such by the Jews, the Samaritans and the Gentiles. For each, there needed to be a kingmaker.

Mary of Bethany was the kingmaker for the Jews.

Pontius Pilate was the kingmaker for the Gentiles.

And for the Samaritans? Yes, another woman. Unnamed. Sinful. Married five times, living immorally with a sixth man.

It cannot be said that Jesus ever picked people who were the epitome of virtue as His kingmakers. He is not simply the One who offers the second chance, He's the One who holds out the high calling and asks us to step into it.

He met the Samaritan woman at a well where she had come to

draw water. It was, in fact, a ceremonial site.

Rehoboam, the son of Solomon, the son of David, had come here to Shechem for his coronation. It's difficult to know why. Perhaps the Gihon spring had dried up, therefore Shechem was chosen not just because of its living—flowing, running—water but because the weight of its historical glory would enhance the young king's prestige.

However, it all went wrong. It was there at Shechem that Rehoboam's pride and arrogance led to the kingdom being torn asunder. Ten tribes rebelled against the house of David, setting in motion a long chain of events that would eventually lead to the peopling of the region by a mixed ethnic group that was known as the Samaritans. The attitude of the peoples of Judea and Samaria was one of mutual contempt.

And Jesus overturned it all with the simplest of requests: '*Give Me a drink.*'

His next remark to the woman's incredulous reminder that He was breaking centuries of rules by talking to her was: '*If you knew the gift of God and who is asking you for a drink, you would have asked Him, and He would have given you living water.*' (John 4:10 BSB)

Notice the allusion to kingship: living water. Jesus cut to the chase almost immediately by mentioning one of the essential requirements for a coronation. That was His agenda: He had come to reunify a long-dismembered kingdom and to restore to the line of David what had been lost to it about nine hundred years previously.

Of course, Jesus was no longer talking about living water as a flowing stream or a bubbling spring, He was talking about Himself as the ultimate refreshment: a spiritual revitalising well of Living Water.

The conversation turned to the Messiah—the Anointed One—the

one designated as king because fragrant oil has been ceremonially poured on his head. The entire dialogue is full of subtle whiffs, referencing deep, unhealed historical wounds. By hinting to an outcast woman that He is the king who wants to appoint her as both His cupbearer and kingmaker, He took an incredible risk. The disgust of Jews and Samaritans for each other had been a pit of septic poison for centuries.

But His risk was rewarded by a corresponding risk on her part.

And so, by introducing the people of her town to the Messiah, this unnamed woman became His kingmaker, His cupbearer, His first evangelist.

It's so easy to fall into the trap of thinking that this was long ago, once and for all time. But no. It's also for the now and not-yet, it's once and future.

There are hearts and souls, trapped in a rebel kingdom and blinded by centuries of prejudice, waiting for a kingmaker to crown the King of kings in their lives. Those hearts and souls might be family, might be friends, might be neighbours, might be strangers. Perhaps one of those hearts, one of those souls, belongs to you.

If that's the case, stop and listen to the whisper. Take heed of the message of the silence.

For the King of kings is asking you to step down from the throne of your life and be His kingmaker when it comes to the kingdom of yourself. It might be a divided self, but He isn't concerned about that.

Throw down your crown and bow before Him, gifting Him all of yourself. Ask Him for the refreshment that comes only from Him as the Living Water, and for the restoration that only comes from Him as the Anointed One.

And then, no matter what your past, don't let it define you. Don't let abuse or rebellion, shame or stupidity, fear or frailty, or even your own sense of unworthiness hold you back. Toss out all the excuses and accept His incomparable invitation. If He calls you to be a kingmaker, like Mary of Bethany or the woman of the well in Samaria, don't think you're disqualified! You might not be a priest like Zadok or a prophet like Nathan but clearly that doesn't matter a jot or a tittle to Jesus.

There's an old saying but a true one: *God doesn't call the qualified, He qualifies the called.*

Take hold of this moment and believe it.

Prayer for myself:

HEAVENLY FATHER, part of me wants to give You the kingdom of myself. Part of me hesitates. Part of me wants to ask You to ascend the throne of my life. Part of me is terrified at losing control.

Just as Jesus asked the Samaritan woman, You say to me: 'Give Me a drink!'

The choice is mine. I can allow You to reunite the kingdom of my heart or I can try to rebuild it myself. I can serve as Your cupbearer or I can silently ignore You. I can give You the polluted water of myself in exchange for Your living water, or I can hold back.

King Jesus, You want me to accept Your invitation to enter Your life. You want me to be born again through the water and spirit that flowed from the wound under Your heart. You want me to live life to the full. You want to cleanse me with the Living Water that comes from You—and You alone.

So, today, I choose life. I choose You.

Wash me clean with the cool living waters of Your Holy Spirit until I am freed of all impurity. Heal me so I can share Your healing with others. Then I can truly say: *It is no longer I who lives but now I live within the heart and life of Jesus.*

Come, King Jesus, come once again. Unite my heart so that all of me wants to give You the kingdom of myself.

I surrender to You, Heavenly Father, and ask You to be my king.

And I ask You to take these words I have spoken and, through the power of the cross of Jesus, grant me the grace of king-making so I can gift to Jesus the kingship of my heart.

In His Name

Amen

Prayer to bless others:

HEAVENLY FATHER, the longer I live the more certain I become that many of my sisters in the Lord are just like me. We have been washed squeaky clean by Your Spirit but, every so often, we contaminate ourselves with poisonous words and actions. We so often fail to keep short accounts with You and ask You to rinse off the defilement covering us.

So we remain prone to repeating that one thing that really does rule supreme in our lives—and that we hide even from ourselves. Yes, we fool ourselves but we cannot fool You. Our inner darkness can lie concealed for a long time but then, when least expected, it suddenly appears. When it's threatened with exposure, it fights to stay hidden and unhealed. And because it's hurt, it sets out to hurt others. Wounded people wound people.

We don't want this, Lord. We want to be true to You, Jesus, Lord and King and Master of all. We want less of us and more of You.

Father, forgive us. We repent and turn back to You. Come, Holy Spirit, come with Your strength and Your power. Come in just the way each of us need You to come so that our repentance is energised by You. Cover us and shield us so we're protected from all that is not of You. Hover over us, Holy Spirit, and draw us into the heart and life of Jesus in fresh and glorious ways.

Thank you, Holy Spirit, for all You have done, all You are doing and all You have yet to do for each of us. I thank You in the holy Name of Jesus of Nazareth and ask You to bless my sisters beyond all they can ask or imagine.

In the name of the precious Living Water.

Amen

2
Woman and Mother: Visionary

2
Woman and Mother: Visionary

Therefore this is His thirst and love-longing, to have us altogether whole in Him.

Julian of Norwich
Revelations of Divine Love

31 OCTOBER 1917. A FLAME-RED sun was setting in a haze of shimmering heat and luminous dust. The shutters of night were falling and, in the distance, a shielding darkness began to settle over the besieged town. The day was almost spent; the last chance to storm the defensive stronghold all but gone.

Twice already that day the horsemen stationed outside the town had been repelled. The German and Turkish troops within the redoubt had fought off their attack, forcing them to retreat into the desert.

But on the dry stony plain, there was no shelter and no water. And without those precious commodities, there were effectively no options. And so, with only the last fire-flecked glow of the setting sun on the tall minaret to guide them, eight hundred mounted infantrymen galloped towards Beersheba and its life-sustaining wells. Horses panting, rifle shots whistling over their heads, machine guns rattling ahead of them, thousands of hooves pounding beneath them, the Anzac light horse brigade charged the Turkish trenches.

The defenders, believing the horsemen would dismount for a hand-to-hand engagement, miscalculated the firing range. But the horses, frenzied with thirst, were determined—so their riders later said—to let nothing stand between them and the water they craved. They leapt the trenches, carrying the Anzacs straight in to the fray.

The taking of Beersheba by allied mounted infantry was lightning sudden. It was so swift the fleeing Turkish army was only able to sabotage a few of its ancient wells. Most remained in intact. The battle cleared the way for the assault on Jerusalem and was to be acclaimed as a significant turning point in the history of nations.

It's not the first time the wells of Beersheba have been so pivotal. In the story of Abraham an explanation is given regarding the name: here, about four thousand years ago, at the well of the oath,[7] Abraham covenanted with the ruler of the kingdom of Gerar.

However, ancient as it is, this is not the first well ever mentioned in Scripture. The very first is a spring[8] in the desert discovered by a slave girl.

The history of sacred wells therefore begins with a woman and perhaps not surprisingly, across the world, a traditional association with the feminine is retained. Whether it's a 'clootie well' in Britain with rags[9] fluttering in nearby trees or a shrine dedicated to 'Our Lady of Tatters' in northern India, whether it's a wishing well glinting with coins or a pin well where pebbles or pins were dropped, a healing well, a holy well or a lady well, the vast majority of sacred wells are considered the domain of women. They are also considered as a place of pilgrimage to fulfil a heart-felt desire. Sometimes, as in Irish folklore, the well has an elderly female guardian who has the power of sovereignty and is able to confer kingship on a chance visitor.[10]

Go back to the darkest roots of civilization and you will find

> *them knotted round some sacred stone or encircling some sacred well.*
>
> GK Chesterton

Dark and deep, cool and mysterious, wells are of course prized for their thirst-quenching refreshment. Over the course of many centuries, they have also for some enigmatic reason, become routinely associated with wisdom. Perhaps that's because bodies of water, like wells, were once considered the gateway between worlds.[11]

That idea is a natural outflow of a divine encounter at the very first well mentioned in Scripture. It was a woman who found this well. She not only named it, she named God in the process. And echoes of her naming rippled down the centuries, like a pebble thrown into water—until Jesus took hold of her 'pebble' and used the naming for Himself.

When I first encountered the idea of God-namers, I was very uncomfortable. It was a revolutionary thought—and just a little bit too far outside my comfort zone. But then I realised I'd better get over my unease because there were far too many instances of God-naming in Scripture to ignore it.

The first name used in relation to God occurs in the opening verse of Genesis. It's 'elohim'; but before we think to ourselves this is God's original revelation to His creation, we need to remember this Scriptural record wasn't put down in writing until the time of Moses. So, in fact, 'elohim' is a retrospective word.

We need to glean a lot more carefully to discover the identity He disclosed to humanity. The very first time God self-reveals in the Bible, He doesn't call Himself 'Yahweh'.[12] Over four hundred years prior to His appearance in the burning bush, He manifested before Abraham:

> *When Abram was ninety-nine years old, the Lord appeared to him and said, 'I am El-Shaddai—"God Almighty." Serve me faithfully and live a blameless life.'*
>
> Genesis 17:1 NLT

Here God He refers to Himself as 'El Shaddai'—usually translated *Almighty*. Actually, however, it seems to be much closer in meaning to *the strong-breasted one*. When God tells Abraham[13] this name, He is speaking of Himself in maternal terms as a nurturer and a provider, as One who cherishes and nurses His children. It has overtones going back to the foundation of time when the Spirit of God brooded over the face of the waters.

Now *El Shaddai* is enormously significant as a self-revelation of God. Yet it's not the first revelation of His name and nature. Thirteen years previously, the first of the God-namers had a visionary encounter with the Lord.

Her name was Hagar. She was a foreigner, a slave, an abused woman.[14] She was apparently nothing more than a commodity in the eyes of her mistress since Sarah never refers to Hagar by name but only as *'that slavewoman'* or *'my handmaiden'*.

Although God had promised Abraham and Sarah a son, it is clear that Sarah had quickly come to the conclusion that she wasn't a viable part of the equation. She was barren. So, for her husband to have an heir born of his own body, she would have to help God keep His word by devising Plan B. She therefore gave her servant to her husband as his second wife, hoping Hagar would get pregnant and produce a son which could be technically attributed to Sarah.

Hagar was soon expecting a child and, as a consequence, she began to look down on Sarah. She might have had nothing in terms of wealth or freedom, but she did have the one and only thing Sarah so passionately wanted: fertility. In reaction, Sarah treated her even more harshly—the abuse intensifying to such a degree that Hagar fled into the wilderness to escape it.

And there, by a spring of water in the desert, the Angel of the Lord found her. The angel's first word, significantly, is her name. The name that Sarah never used.

Is it any wonder she called God '*the Living One who sees me*'?

To be seen and acknowledged is such a profound need of the human heart that, when people who have been traumatised by childhood abuse are asked if they'd rather have been ignored than mistreated, almost all say they'd choose brutality over neglect. Somewhere deep within we recognise a hierarchy of cruelty and we'd rather be beaten than suffer the soul-wrenching loneliness of moving through life entirely invisible to others.

Echoes of Hagar's naming reverberate through time. Her visionary insight, '*The Living One who sees me*', has the same sort of connotations as a divine title declared by another God-namer just a few decades later. When Abraham has climbed Mount Moriah to sacrifice Isaac as a burnt offering to God, the Angel of the Lord appears again. And again, his first word is Abraham's name. As the angel directs Abraham not to lay a hand on Isaac, a ram is discovered, caught in a thicket.

Recognising this provision from God can be offered as a substitute for his son, Abraham called El Shaddai by a new name: 'Yahweh Yireh'. This is often given as Jehovah Jireh, and is usually translated *the One who provides*. However, it is much closer in meaning to *the One who sees my need*.

How subtly this harks back to Hagar's naming: the Living One who sees me. And lest we make the mistake of thinking the names are not really connected, Scripture itself stitches them neatly together.

Hagar had named the spring in the desert where she had encountered God as Beer Lahai Roi: *the well of the Living One who sees me*.

The next time we hear of this well, Isaac suddenly and mysteriously appears there. When Abraham left Mount Moriah for home in Beersheba, we hear about his servants going with him. But there's no mention of Isaac. We never hear of him returning with his father. For a time in the story, he's so completely invisible it's unclear what happened after the Angel of the Lord told Abraham to put down his knife.

The next time we hear of Isaac—much later, in fact, since he plays no part in the story of Sarah's death and burial—he is at Beer Lahai Roi, *the well of the Living One who sees me*. He has camped for a time at the very same spring where Hagar met God.

Perhaps, in the final analysis, like Hagar, Isaac needed something far greater than provision: a sense of being seen by God.

The very first vision of God's nature was given to a desperate and broken woman. She doesn't make it into the long list of heroes of the faith in Hebrews 11 but she proclaimed a mystery later endorsed by Abraham, Moses and Jesus.

In naming the well 'Beer Lahai Roi'—the well of the Living One who sees me—she also names God. Look at how her declaration calls to mind the name God disclosed to Moses at the burning bush. Yes, in addition to reminding us of Yahweh Yireh, the name Abraham gave to God, it should also bring to mind, I AM Who I AM. This name, given to Moses, can also be translated I will be who I will be, as well as the Existing One or the Ever-living One.

That last variation, *Ever-living One*, confirms to us that Hagar discerned an essential truth about God.

God's self-revelation to Moses doesn't make Moses a God-namer. Let's carefully distinguish between the declarations God makes about Himself and the revelations He gives to us so we can choose to use the insight His Spirit gives. David names God as *Shepherd* and Gideon names Him as *Peace*. Abraham goes for a second strike and names Him 'El Olam', the *Eternal God* or *Everlasting Lord*.

Moses only becomes part of this company when, after a battle with the Amalekites, he calls God 'Yahweh Nissi', *the Lord my banner*. But the disclosure he received at Mount Sinai regarding God's identity, *Ever-living One*, is like a brush-by of that pebble Hagar has skipped across the waters of time. God later told Moses:

> *I appeared to Abraham, to Isaac, and to Jacob as El-Shaddai—'God Almighty'—but I did not reveal my name, Yahweh, to them.*
>
> Exodus 6:3 NLT

Hagar didn't know the name 'Yahweh' either but she had looked up long enough to see sufficient of the truth of His divine nature to call Him 'Lahai Roi'.

The pebble skipping across the waters of time finally reached its destination. The scene by the well in the wilderness evokes many moments through salvation history but perhaps none more strongly than the encounter between Jesus and Samaritan woman. She too was a stranger, a foreigner, a wary and marginalised woman. She too came to a well and was astonished to be seen. Her guarded heart opened as she realised she was seen by God!

And God came to visit her, not just as the Living One but as the Living Water. Jesus did not despise her broken, lowly position but encouraged her to look up and see—and, in seeing, recognise that He was the Messiah. He acknowledged her, engaged her in conversation, treated her as worthy of respect. As we have seen in the last chapter, He asked her to be His cupbearer and He established her as His kingmaker. But cupbearer and kingmaker were not the only roles He summoned her into; He also asked her to be a visionary—to be seen, and in being seen, to see.

What happens between Hagar and the Angel of the Lord at the

well on the road to Shur is prophetic of Jesus encountering the woman of Samaria at the well on the road to Sychar. Both incidents tell us that God doesn't wait for His visionaries to come to Him. He goes out to meet us wherever we're hiding, wherever we've run. And it doesn't matter how broken we are, how low we've sunk, how much we've been battered and bruised, beaten and betrayed—none of that is relevant to Him. He calls us by name and asks us to look up, so we can see Him—and so can see our own worth in His eyes.

> *Remember who you are, despite the bad things that are happening to you. Because those bad things aren't you.*
>
> Colleen Hoover, *Hopeless*

He calls us to be visionaries and see the worth in others as well, even those who have battered and betrayed us. He calls us to renew our vision when betrayal has blinded us—as He did many years later for Hagar.[15] He calls us to help draw forth from others, as from a spring of water, life and truth, love and joy.

> *There are no ordinary people. You have never talked to a mere mortal. Nations, cultures, arts, civilisations—these are mortal, and their life is to ours as the life of a gnat. But it is immortals whom we joke with, work with, marry, snub, and exploit—immortal horrors or everlasting splendours.*
>
> CS Lewis, *The Weight of Glory*

Jesus calls us to take His hand and to walk with Him along the dark, tangled path into the secret heart of our own crushed spirit. He wants us to keep going, with Him by our side, until we find the ancient well where our hopes and dreams have drowned. As we approach it, He calls on us to tear down the ragged wishes fluttering on the branches around the well and surrender them to Him. He calls us express our deep sorrow for trying to buy the desire of our heart from Him with a token thrown into the well. Such votive offerings fall forever, never reaching bottom—and they poison the well, twisting our hearts in the process so we mistake wishes for faith. Like Sarah with Plan B, we try to help God fulfil His promises and so wind up creating our own toxic pit of jealousy, frustration, cruelty and manipulation.

> *Keep your heart with all diligence, for out of it is the wellspring of life.*
>
> Proverbs 4:23 WEB

Here the Hebrew word for *wellspring* also means *boundary* or *border*. God gives us boundaries and also asks us to put them in place so we will receive the consummation of our heart's desire, not be consumed by it. And in that delight, when we see and are seen, He calls us to gift others with the same: He asks us to give sight to the spiritually blind. First by seeing them, and acknowledging them, being present heart-to-heart with them, using their names.

But, to begin, we need to see ourselves as we truly are.

> *Remember that the dullest most uninteresting person you can talk to may one day be a creature which, if you saw it now, you would be strongly tempted to worship, or else a horror and a corruption such as you now meet, if at all, only in a nightmare. All day long we are, in some degree helping each other to one or the other of these destinations.*
>
> CS Lewis, *The Weight of Glory*

It would be neat if God wrapped up our calling and put it into a box conveniently labelled KINGMAKER or CUPBEARER or VISIONARY. So it would all be nice and tidy and we'd know for sure His purpose for us. We'd be able to confidently answer why He created us and state the meaning of our lives.

But He doesn't do that. He so often calls us to fulfil more than one role. He also calls us to work with other believers and commands a blessing when we do.

> *Look how good and how pleasant it is*
> *when brothers live together in unity!…*
> *For there the Lord commanded his blessing—*
> *life everlasting.*

Psalm 133:1;3 ISV

On 31 October 1917, eight hundred horsemen from Australia thundered across the dusty plains towards the place where Hagar had lived with Abraham and Sarah so many millennia previously.[16] History was made that day as Beersheba was liberated and the first wedge was driven into centuries of Ottoman domination of the Holy Land. Did those foreign troopers, ordinary sun-bronzed men who cursed the heat and the dust, know they were riding into a watershed moment in time? Almost certainly not.

History was made the day a foreign slave fled from the domination of Sarah and met the Angel of the Lord. She blazed a trail others followed and then endorsed. Did Hagar know she was heading straight into a watershed moment in time? Again, almost certainly not.

God calls us, in this time, to be history-makers too. And we're not going to recognise the watershed moments until long after, if at all. So how do we fulfil that high calling, if we don't know the way? If we've got our heads down fighting a battle or if our eyes are lowered because we've been bruised and crushed so heavily we don't dare raise them?

We simply meet Him by faith and ask Him to take us to the wellspring of our heart; and there we look up. So we can see and be seen, so we can name and be named.

So we can become visionaries.

Prayer for myself:

HEAVENLY FATHER, forgive me for my lack of understanding into how often my own actions affect me so deeply. My destiny is not nearly affected as much, Father, by what has happened to me as the way I have reacted to what has happened.

I blame others and avoid my own responsibility to respond to Your call for repentance. I blame myself and let others off the hook, side-stepping Your call for forgiveness.

I even blame You, Father. I fume to myself: 'How could You let this happen to me!? You could have stopped it! Why didn't You? Don't You care?'

Open my eyes to the need to repent of my blindness and to withdraw my judgments of You. Teach me, Father, to discern what is my responsibility and what is not. Teach me when to forgive and when to repent. Teach me how to take responsibility for all I think and say and do.

Father, I am so slow to learn. Let me embrace with open arms all that You have in store for me and let me acknowledge how important I am in Your sight. Make me aware that I may be the only image of Your Son that many people will see this week. Give me an awareness of how vital it is that I make You known wherever I go. Make me aware that I really am a signpost to Your Kingdom on this earth wherever I am and whatever I do.

Teach me, Father, that no matter what I have done, I can at any time sit at Your feet or snuggle up in Your arms. Show me how I can rest and refresh safely enfolded in the arms of my Daddy.

Jesus told me to call You Abba—Daddy. You are not distant—You are my Daddy. You have blessed me with every heavenly blessing. Let me praise and thank You and rejoice and be glad and enjoy Your presence forever.

In the name of Jesus

Amen

Prayer to bless others:

FATHER, there are no 'others' in this great and wonderful world You gave us—only friends or neighbours we have not yet met. And You are their Daddy too. This really does make us one family. Sometimes we bicker and sometimes we hurt and harm each other terribly, but that does not make us less Your children.

What You do for me, You also do for them. Your rain falls on the just and the unjust.

Heavenly Father, I come before you with my sisters. We are aware that, as individuals and as a family, we have dishonoured You. We have disobeyed You and treated You with disrespect. We have ignored You and have quarreled among ourselves.

Father, we repent and ask Your forgiveness for our daily disrespect and dishonour. We withdraw our judgment of You for the times we blamed You for the mess we had brought upon ourselves. Father, forgive us for our blindness. We thank you for eyes to see the beauty that is all around us and in each other. We thank You for ears that hear the wisdom of Your word.

Please forgive us for the times we have overlooked Your provision and failed to see and hear. And Lord God, forgive us for our failure to tell of You to a people in need of You in this thirsty and starving world.

Despite this, we can at any time come to You and be a fully accepted daughter of the King and a sister of Your Son, Jesus. We can be secure in Your loving embrace. What a privilege! What an honour! What an awesome God You are! Thank You. Thank You. You are a God lavish in grace and mercy.

Father, I ask You to bless beyond measure my sisters in the Lord with honour—and my brothers too. Not because any of us are worthy but because Your Son paid the price that we might be counted worthy in Your sight.

In His Name.

Amen.

3
Woman and Mother: Navigator

3
Woman and Mother: Navigator

HAGAR'S STORY IS EXCEPTIONAL BUT not an exception—there are other women like her in the Scriptural record. They too were pioneers, blazing a new trail, resetting the direction on a spiritual compass. Yet Hagar's role as a forerunner tends to fade into obscurity because she's not the mother of a child of the covenant. Rather she's the mother of an outcast.

Still let's not overlook the fact that God twice made a personal appearance to her. Much like, in a later age, He twice appeared to Solomon—something that was seen as an incomparable privilege.[17]

Hagar's story is not only a changepoint for her, it's also prophetic of God's future dealing with the Gentiles. Just as non-Jews were destined to be grafted into the family of God through faith, so Hagar came to a faith-knowledge of the one true God through her association with the tiny family God had chosen to set apart for Himself.

However, there's no denying that, when we're thinking of radical innovators in Scripture, it's unlikely our minds will turn to a woman. Somehow the wives and widows, mothers and maidens, have fallen into the cracks of history and become invisible. Yet their actions are just as plain on the page as any of the more lionised male heroes of the faith. We've been unfortunately conditioned to think that, in salvation history, the main role of women was stay quietly in the background and bear children.

Certainly that would be an easy impression to receive, given the extreme emphasis on the barrenness of women in the Scriptural record: Sarah, Rebecca, Rachel, Hannah, Elizabeth, Samson's mother, the women of Gerar. But this is probably to miss the point of those stories: it was barrenness that drove so many of these women to seek God. To seek Him fervently and desperately.

And, when it comes to the crunch, the stories of those women who were easily able to conceive are actually no different. For each of them, there was a crisis that drove them to fervently and desperately seek God.

Two of the most significant of these women are Leah and Hannah. One unloved, the other deeply loved. One crazy for her husband's affection, the other secure in it. One able to bear children with ease, the other heartbroken at her childlessness. So different, yet so much the same: both finally seek God in their troubles. And in doing so, they become trailblazers in their own right. Hannah, in fact, joins the ranks of the God-namers.

However, before we look at her story, let's examine that of Leah. She was the older sister of Rachel and daughter of Laban. Rachel was so lovely to look at that Jacob was smitten at first glance and fell so head-over-heels he was willing to work for seven years to have her as his wife. However, Laban tricked him into marrying Leah first—and perhaps Jacob never forgave her for her part in the deception. Certainly she spent years striving to gain a small share in his affection, hoping that the children she was bearing would gain her some fondness in his eyes.

How many women have been like her across the ages, thinking

that their marriages will change for the better when children come along?

Leah never seemed to get any emotional traction with Jacob; even her children were discounted. Jacob made this remarkable statement in Genesis 42:38 NLT which revealed his inner attitude towards them:

> *'My son will not go down with you. His brother Joseph is dead, and he is all I have left. If anything should happen to him on your journey, you would send this grieving, white-haired man to his grave.'*

When he said, *'my son... all I have left...'* he was referring to Benjamin. It's as if he has no children other than the sons of Rachel—Joseph, whom he believed was dead, and Benjamin. The argument which climaxed with this statement was about his second son Simeon who, at this point, was in prison in Egypt. All it would have taken to free him was for Benjamin to show up, but Jacob wouldn't let it happen. His words and his actions say that Benjamin is precious to him; Simeon is worthless.

Jacob's favouritism towards Rachel's children and his almost callous dismissal of Leah's offspring seem to reflect his attitude towards their mothers. He simply didn't care for Leah, despite all her efforts to win a crumb of affection from him. It took years for her to realise nothing would change. When she first bore Jacob a son, she was so obviously hopeful. Naming the child Reuben, she said, *'The Lord has seen my affliction. Surely my husband will love me now.'*

Hear the desperate yearning in those words: 'Surely my husband will love me now.' But her hopes were dashed. Over the next few years, her optimism rose repeatedly with the birth of each new son, only to be crushed back down.

> *Again she conceived and gave birth to a son, and she said, 'Because the Lord has heard that I am unloved, He has given*

> *me this son as well.' So she named him Simeon.*
>
> *Once again Leah conceived and gave birth to a son, and she said, 'Now at last my husband will become attached to me, because I have borne him three sons.' So he was named Levi.*
>
> Genesis 29:32–34 BSB

Then, at long last, she realised the truth. Jacob wasn't going to change. He was so totally besotted with her sister he would never have eyes for anyone else. Leah could have become embittered at this point; she could have taken out her anger and frustration on those around her. She could, like so many of us, have pointed the finger of blame at God and held Him responsible for her anguish.

Instead she does something no one in the Bible is ever recorded as doing previously.

> *Once more, she conceived and gave birth to a son and said, 'This time I will praise the Lord.' So she named him Judah.*
>
> Genesis 29:35 BSB

She praised God.

She raised her hands to heaven and gave thanks. Praise is mentioned so often in Scripture it's easy to overlook its first appearance.[18] It happens when Leah gives birth for a fourth time.

Take particular note of the circumstances: it's not in celebration of a great victory; not in remembrance of some glorious fulfilment of a promise; not when a cherished dream at last comes true. It's when a disappointed woman chooses to turn to God in her brokenness and her pain and give thanks anyway.

As she changed direction, she became the navigator and bridge-builder for the future. For it is through the line of Judah that Jesus, the Messiah, would eventually come.

> *Island calls to island across the silence, and once, in trust, the real words come, a bridge is built and love is done—not sentimental, emotional love, but love that is pontifex, bridge-builder. Love that speaks the holy and healing word which is: God be with you, stranger who are no stranger. I wish you well. The islands become an archipelago, a continent, become a kingdom whose name is the Kingdom of God.*
>
> Frederick Buechner, *The Hungering Dark*

In ancient times, people thought the making of a bridge was such a miraculous skill it must be inspired by the gods. A pontifex—bridge-builder—was almost a sacred title and the greatest were treated as close to divine.

Make no mistake, Leah built a bridge to heaven. Her husband might have had a vision of a ladder with angels ascending and descending on it, but Leah's expression of faith is no less significant. She may not have known that God inhabits the praises of His people, but her acknowledgement of Him was a gateway into her life and into the situation. Her legacy is that of the first person ever mentioned as praising God—a woman who surrendered her hope of earthly favour and who put on record her thankfulness for heavenly favour.

Another pioneer—innovator, trailblazer, pathfinder and bridge-builder—is Hannah. She was the mother of Samuel, whose life spans the transitional era from the judges to the kings. The tribal society of her time sought spiritual and political direction from the priesthood at Shiloh. But that government was corrupt—the high priest Eli was negligent and his sons depraved. Scripture calls them 'sons of Belial', a phrase often translated *worthless fellows* but actually indicating they worshipped a demonic power.[19] The defilement over the sanctuary had led to silence from God. His voice was no longer being heard in the land. And as the desecration of His house became worse, He withdrew His presence and, with it, His protection.

But His eyes, which continually range throughout the earth to find those who are committed to Him, had come to rest on a person who was willing to invite His intervention. Perhaps, from Hannah's point of view, her desperate prayer was only to relieve her immediate circumstances, but in God's providence, it was for the entire nation.

Hannah's misery revolved around her inability to have a child. Although she was deeply loved by her husband, she was taunted and belittled by his other wife who had given birth to an entire brood of children.

> *To belittle, you have to be little.*
>
> Kahlil Gibran

In her heartache, Hannah went to God. Her husband had taken the family to worship at the tabernacle at Shiloh and Hannah used the opportunity to approach God as closely as she could. She went to the door and, shuddering with grief, she made a vow to Yahweh Sabaoth, *the Lord of Hosts*. She is the first person to describe God this way, the first to beg for help from the Commander of the Armies of Heaven.[20]

As she was there by the door, trembling in anguish of soul, the high priest Eli spotted her. As she shook and mumbled under her breath, he assumed she'd been drinking too much. It would have been an easy mistake, given the licentious environment at Shiloh.

Unknown to her, unknown to Eli, her prayer is the means of breakthrough Yahweh Sabaoth has long desired to give to His people. Things were about to change—though certainly not as quickly as the people of Israel would have liked.

And definitely not as quickly as our 'gimme-gimme' generation! We want an instant solution—we wouldn't have wanted to wait for as long as Hannah took to conceive, bear a son, wean him and escort him to the tabernacle. The end of our wait still wouldn't have been over, because then there were the years of Samuel's tutelage under Eli until he heard from God—and still more years until he was old enough to take over when Eli and his sons all died on the same day.

Yes, we're talking decades before the abuse and corruption that was an everyday reality at Shiloh was swept away in a single day.

Hannah was the innovator who set all this in motion. She was the navigator who instigated a change in direction. Unless we remember the genealogy that opens the two books of Samuel and understand their significance, we miss the magnitude of this change.

> *Now there was a certain man from Ramathaim-zophim from the hill country of Ephraim, and his name was Elkanah the son of Jeroham, the son of Elihu, the son of Tohu, the son of Zuph, an Ephraimite.*
>
> 1 Samuel 1:1 NASB

Now the genealogy of Hannah's husband, Elkanah, as it's presented here is somewhat misleading. It gives the impression that his son Samuel comes from the tribe of Ephraim, not the tribe of Levi. However 1 Chronicles 6:33–38, in listing the musicians who served in the temple, reveals that Samuel was the twentieth generation from Levi.[21]

Nevertheless, throughout the history chronicled in 1 and 2 Samuel, there is no hint of this ancestry. The record seems determined to conceal his bloodline, emphatically repeating the name Ephraim in the first verse—thus giving the impression Samuel belongs to another tribe entirely. Be that as it may, one thing is clear: no matter what way we look at it, Samuel is definitely *not* descended from Aaron.

God has set up the circumstances for a boy to be effectively adopted into the line of Aaron, rather than be born into it. The curse on the house of Eli for honouring his sons more than he honoured

God went on for generations. Eli did not discipline his sons but allowed them to indulge in all manner of degrading practices at the tabernacle.

As Paul put it so succinctly over a millennia later:

> *Do not be deceived: God is not mocked, for whatever one sows, that will he also reap.*
>
> Galatians 6:7 ESV

However, God had no intention of leaving the His chosen people leaderless, without a high priest, without someone who could hear His voice and intercede on their behalf. So He planned an exception: He planned to bring to birth a prophet and a priest who would transition His people from the period of the judges into the era of the kings.

Still, as in a later age when His only-begotten Son was ready to come into the world, He waited on the choice of a woman. It's no coincidence that the Thanksgiving Song of Hannah is so similar to the Magnificat[22] of Mary:

> *My heart exults in the Lord;*
> *My horn is exalted in the Lord,*
> *My mouth speaks boldly against my enemies,*
> *Because I rejoice in Your salvation.*
>
> *There is no one holy like the Lord,*
> *Indeed, there is no one besides You,*
> *Nor is there any rock like our God.*
>
> *Boast no more so very proudly,*
> *Do not let arrogance come out of your mouth;*
> *For the Lord is a God of knowledge,*
> *And with Him actions are weighed.*
>
> *The bows of the mighty are shattered,*

But the feeble gird on strength.

Those who were full hire themselves out for bread,
But those who were hungry cease to hunger.
Even the barren gives birth to seven,
But she who has many children languishes.

The Lord kills and makes alive;
He brings down to Sheol and raises up.

The Lord makes poor and rich;
He brings low, He also exalts.

He raises the poor from the dust,
He lifts the needy from the ash heap
To make them sit with nobles,
And inherit a seat of honour;
For the pillars of the earth are the Lord's,
And He set the world on them.

He keeps the feet of His godly ones,
But the wicked ones are silenced in darkness;
For not by might shall a man prevail.

Those who contend with the Lord will be shattered;
Against them He will thunder in the heavens,
The Lord will judge the ends of the earth;
And He will give strength to His king,
And will exalt the horn of His anointed.

1 Samuel 2:1–10 NAS

It's clear from this song that Hannah was a prophet. Unacknowledged, true, but notice that she specifically prophesied the coming kingship and the number of her own children as well as, more generally, the fall of the house of Eli. She was also the first to mention 'the Lord's anointed' and thus to reveal that the Lord has a Messiah![23]

Her influence is still apparent today. She is credited by some traditions within Judaism with inventing a swaying form of prayer called shuckling.[24] The grief-stricken trembling and shaking that accompanied her plea to God has persisted through the ages.

Debbie Lustig noted that, at a New Year[25] service she attended where there were many infants present, the rhythm of rocking in prayer matched the rhythm of rocking the newborn babies.[26]

That's a beautiful image. In a very real sense we need to prepare room in our heart for a newborn before a child can be conceived. As we look at the story of Hannah, we may think she had room to spare, but actually she didn't. See, Hannah just wanted to conceive a child. However heaven wanted her to conceive a move of God. That requires a lot more space in the heart, and a different kind of thinking.

Could she welcome God's plan into her life, knowing there'd be thorns as well as fragrance? That's often our dilemma too.

Could she surrender what her own idea of motherhood would look like? God knew what Hannah did not. She might have suspected destruction was looming, but not the degree of it. The House of Eli had to reap what it had sown. A curse was proceeding inexorably towards fulfilment. The sons of Eli had chosen Belial, so it would be Belial who would attend them in war, not Yahweh Sabaoth.

The future of the entire nation actually hung on a fine thread at this point. There would have been no Israel, had Hannah chosen differently. Not only was the priesthood about to be totally wiped out in a single day, the Ark of the Covenant—the sign of God's presence with His people—was about to be taken in battle by the Philistines. The loss of the Ark only reflected the spiritual reality: Yahweh Sabaoth had departed while His priests were worshipping Belial. Yet they expected Him to be able to whistle up at their convenience when they needed Him to head the battle array of the armies of Israel.

How often do we do the same? How often do we cling to worthless idols—only to try to wheedle our way with God in a crisis? And even blame Him when He doesn't jump to attention and solve our problems with a majestic, dismissive wave of His hand?

Like Hannah, we need to make room in our heart for more than our own desires.

God loves us and unquestionably has plans for us which include fulfilling the desires of our hearts—yet His blessings are not for ourselves alone. They are given so we can be a blessing to others.

To be navigators, trailblazers, pathfinders, bridge-builders, instigators, forerunners—yes, and even God-namers!

Prayer for myself:

HEAVENLY FATHER, I confess and repent of the fact that when my life was going well I did not seek You with my whole being. But I found You when my life was at its lowest point. When I had done all that I possibly could. I had often prayed for You to heal my life but I failed miserably to move myself aside and surrender to Your ministrations so that You could heal and restore me. When things could get no worse and I was ready to knock on the door of the psychiatric hospital, I cried: 'I can do no more. I abdicate as queen of my life. I cannot continue. Over to You, God!'

And I heard a quiet gentle voice say: 'Gladly, dearheart. What took you so long?'

I have been my own worst enemy. I am sorry and ask Your forgiveness. It was my wilful, do-it-my-way nature that caused me so much pain for so long. Father, I come before you today and confess my stubbornness and I ask you to heal any remnant of pride or obstinacy that remains. I ask Your help to overcome a spirit of independence. Rebuke that spirit for me, Lord. At one time I considered independence to be my greatest asset but now know You require me to be corporate—to be interdependent and part of a like-minded team committed to You and to each other. Show me how to take my rightful place in Your Body and to work for Kingdom values.

Father, pour the soothing balm of Your Holy Spirit on my wounds and on my memories. Let me experience the peace that comes from being one with You as I re-commit to living my life in tune with the heart of Jesus and for Your greater glory.

Amen.

Prayer to bless others:

HEAVENLY FATHER, I come before You and pray with and for my sisters in the faith. So many of us were seduced into believing lies by our parents, teachers and elders. They knew no better and meant no harm but what they taught was not Your truth.

They taught us never to trust others—that if we wanted something done well to do it ourselves.

They taught us that big girls don't cry so we learned to stuff our emotions. Then they taught us that, to get our own way, tears were expedient. So we learned to manipulate emotions.

They taught us it's a sin to be angry but didn't show us how to express anger properly. They didn't tell us that emotions like rage never die—they fester over time and emerge in volcanic outbursts or serious illness.

Abba, these beliefs and many like them were all lies of the enemy. They are not in accord with Your Word. But we believed them. The effect on our lives has been devastating. Lord, we forgive those who taught us. We forgive those who gave us the idea You are a big policeman always on the watch for the tiniest mistake. We renounce these lies and reject them as a tool of Satan.

Father, we accept Your forgiveness and thank You. We ask for the grace to live according to Your will. We acknowledge that we all need help at times, that's okay to be sad when something distressing happens and it's healthy to be angry at injustice and unfair treatment.

Teach us, Father, that it's not anger that is wrong but how we express it—that if we hold on to it unduly and nurture it, it becomes unforgiveness and bitterness. Forgive us, Father—we are sorry. We repent. And we ask Jesus to empower these words of repentance.

Father, thank You for the flow of grace and peace You gift us when we live according to Your truth.

In Jesus' Name.

Amen.

4
Woman and Mother: Sentinel

4
Woman and Mother: Sentinel

'Unless the Lord keepeth the city, the watchman guardeth in vain.'

John F. Kennedy's unspoken
words in Dallas, 23 November 1963
Quoted by Anne Sexton, *Keeping the City*

MANY YEARS AGO, I FINISHED a deeply satisfying romantic novel and, as I sat back in that glowy emotional moment, a horrid thought struck me. I never felt such profound satisfaction when I read Scripture. Surely in the gospel happiest-of-happy-ever-afters I could expect to experience an even greater rush of joy than in a work of fiction, however well-crafted?

I pondered this and wondered if there was something wrong in me. I didn't find Scripture boring but I found it flat, devoid of poignant moments that touched my heart. So I said to God, 'I think I'm missing what is really there. Somehow the fun and the laughter, the romance and the wonder have all been ironed out. Can You show me how to read so I'm not oblivious to it all?'

So He did.

It took a long time. That's because I'm a slow learner. And His lessons almost always revolved around the question: 'Don't you think this scene is a bit *un*natural?'

Not natural or supernatural, but *un*natural. He began to direct my attention to scenes that don't fit in either category—stories where there's nothing overtly miraculous going on but they're definitely not ordinary either. He restored my wonder, my curiosity, my awe, allowing me to ask questions that—to start with—were unanswerable.

One of these first questions centred on the story of the two disciples on the road to Emmaus. And my thought was this: it's implausible, you know, that the first thing any person would do on coming back from the dead is to take a casual walk into the countryside to meet a couple of randoms never previously mentioned in the story. The natural reaction of any person coming back from the dead would surely, surely and surely again be to first reassure friends and family—to alleviate their heartbreak, tears and grief. Not to take a stroll out beyond the 'burbs.

The Emmaus incident is, at least on the surface, profoundly *un*natural. Yet since it's clearly on the top of Jesus' agenda for that particular day as soon as He returns from the Father, it must be superlatively important. So what is this story *really* about? It is of course charming and heart-warming; it has a touch of suspense as well as comedy; it's a refreshing aftermath to the treachery and political machinations surrounding Jesus' grisly death. But all that isn't enough to highlight it so prominently.

Now, of course, as to meaning—an entire kaleidoscope can be found by honing in on different aspects of the story. I'm just going to choose one: the appointment of watchmen. One of whom, according to early Christian writings, was a woman.

And her name was... wait for it. Mary.

That's probably not a surprise. It seems to be the most common female name in Judea and Galilee in the first century.[27]

Early accounts identify the unnamed disciple who was with Cleopas on the road to Emmaus as his wife. She appears to have been one of the three Marys who maintained a vigil at the foot of the cross during the crucifixion of Jesus.[28]

Suddenly the story begins to make sense. The unnatural aspects of it start to fade. The two disciples aren't random at all; Jesus made it His top priority to comfort the very women who stood by Him when He was dying. He spoke to the Magdalene in the garden; He spoke to Mary, His own mother, later that evening—and, in the meantime, He spoke to the third Mary and her husband on the road to Emmaus.

Albert Einstein allegedly said: 'Coincidence is God's way of remaining anonymous.'

And remain anonymous was certainly what Jesus did throughout most of this episode. Is there, however, any significance in the fact that the women at the Cross were (coincidentally and confusingly) named Mary?

I don't think so.

Let's back up a week. As we saw in the first chapter, Mary of Bethany was the kingmaker who anointed Jesus with oil and who washed Him with the living water of her tears. Now, although I previously quoted Luke's version of the story, I want to add a small detail attested by both Matthew and Mark. Jesus makes this comment about Mary's action in anointing Him:

> *'Assuredly, I say to you, wherever this gospel is preached in the whole world, what this woman has done will also be told as a memorial to her.'*

Mark 4:19 NKJV

The story of Mary the kingmaker is a memorial! A monument created in order that future generations will not forget a special moment in history. Memorials are about memory. And perhaps it is a coincidence or perhaps it is simply God working anonymously, but the name 'Mary' is a branch of the same tree of words to which 'memory' and 'memorial' belong. Also part of this tree is 'Samaria', which means *watchtower*.

In fact, both Samaritan and Magdalene mean *of the watchtower*.

A watchtower is a place where a sentinel stands guard. In ancient times, they were high lookouts where keepers of the watch maintained their vigil. These keepers were charged with the protection of cities by remaining on the alert for enemies. Sometimes they were stationed in vineyards to keep watch for marauding wild animals.

These sentinels need to be interpreters of signs and signals; they need to be able to discern accurately—even from a distance—friend from foe in order to give timely warnings. They need to recognise suspicious activity but also be able to distinguish the approach of a harmless stranger from a disguised enemy. The finest watchmen of Scripture had acquired the skill to recognise people by the way they ran or even drove a chariot.

Ironically, both Mary Magdalene and Mary, the wife of Cleopas, fail the first test of a watchman: they don't recognise the resurrected Jesus when they see Him.

> '*Go, set a watchman; let him announce what he sees.*'
>
> Isaiah 21:6 ESV

This is the instruction of the Lord to the priest and prophet Isaiah.

Our high priest, Jesus—who is also a prophet—set His own watchmen, and mysteriously the appointments seemed to include more women than men. For it is as watchmen, sentinels, protections and guardians that the Marys were called. But, you may ask, what were they watching over?

Mary Magdalene gives us the clue: she found Jesus in the garden. The 'garden' or the 'vineyard' in Scripture symbolised inheritance. Yes, these women were appointed to guard the inheritance of God's Word. As their names suggest, they were called to be living witnesses of His story and protect its memory against future exaggeration or embellishment.

The Mary who trod the road to Emmaus was there as Jesus explained how the Tanakh—the Law, the Prophets and the Writings—testified to His life and His death. She was listening as He indicated the words and the ways in which He had fulfilled all of the ancient prophecies and had embodied the signs and symbols of all of the Feasts. Furthermore, not to be less than thorough in any aspect of messianic expectation, He'd also fulfilled quite a few traditions as well that had grown up over the ages.

Because she'd been present as an eyewitness to His death, Mary could verify how His explanations fitted the facts. Thus she and her husband became the official repositories of the only divinely sanctioned interpretation of Scripture. Jesus had personally explained to them how it all applied to Him.

Thus they were appointed guardians of the inheritance of the Word of God. The earliest Christian understanding of prophecy as it pertained to Jesus would have to have passed the plumbline test of all the details He had revealed to them.

So too Mary Magdalene, the kingmaker and the living memorial, was a similar guardian: her testimony to the resurrection was the most detailed, the most comprehensive, the most encompassing. John didn't see Jesus until He appeared late in the evening in the Upper Room. Peter apparently did see Him but the details are obscure.

Instead it was Mary, Mary and Mary who become the guardians of memory—along with Salome as well as Cleopas, just in case you might conclude that you can't be a watchman for Jesus unless your name happens to be Mary!

Mary the mother of Jesus was, after all, a similar guardian. She was custodian of the memories surrounding His birth and she testified to them so other aspects of His fulfilment of prophecy would be on record. And perhaps too, we could regard her as a kingmaker in a different way since she gave birth to the King of kings.

All this indicates it's unlikely we're ever called to just one role. Jesus may summon us to be His kingmaker as well as a sentinel, along with a navigator and a God-namer.

The office of watchman is one of great responsibility:

> *If the watchman sees the enemy coming and doesn't sound the alarm to warn the people, he is responsible for their captivity.*
>
> Ezekiel 33:6 NLT

This is a tough calling. Because in today's world, it's rarely barbarians at the gates who are the invaders. Rather watchmen are called to rouse the slumbering church from more subtle and stealthy attacks: that of trendy ideas marching in under a banner of cultural relevance.

Jesus was never relevant; He was revolutionary. If He'd been culturally relevant, it would have been the three Marks who were appointed His first watchmen, not the Marys.

Are you called as a watchman? Don't, for a moment, think that womanhood disqualifies you! Simply ask the Lord to season you and engrave these credentials on your heart:

vigilance

faithfulness

discernment.

Prayer for myself:

HEAVENLY FATHER, Abba, Daddy God. I come before You and ask You to awaken and call to life in me the very purpose for which I was born. I confess that so often I have been reluctant to say, 'Here I am, Lord, send me.' Too often it has been: 'Here I am, Lord, send someone else.'

I am hesitant and wary. Deep down I am afraid that You might ask me to move out of my comfort zone into strange and unfamiliar territoy. Yet I want to be like those first century women who followed You with their whole heart and mind, soul and spirit.

Forgive me, Abba, and speak courage to my heart so that I move and live and have my being in You. You understand and know me in ways in do not know myself.

Strip away the stains and the dross and purify my heart so that its song is one of ceaseless praise to You. Reveal my authentic self to me so I can follow You with head held high. Make me aware that I am just like the three Marys and that I am a beloved daughter of the King of Kings. O happy day!

Prayer to bless others:

HEAVENLY FATHER, the mothers and grandmothers, sisters and aunts, of the next generation, have a daunting task ahead. Without You it is impossible. I pray for these precious women to be alert—ever watchful for the tricks of the enemy.

You have made us in Your image to be women of grace, dignity and honour. Write that truth on our hearts. Give us a sense of our own dignity and convict us deep in our spirit that You do not make junk.

Abba, teach us and give us the ability to call to life the very best that our children can be. Show us how to be alert to and aware of the differences in each individual, and to note each has their own strengths and weaknesses. Teach them they really are special—but never special at the expense of anyone else. The specialness lies in the fact that each person is unique and is your image-bearer. When You made each of us, You were thrilled and You threw away the mould. No two persons are ever the same. We are unique with a unique role to bring Your Kingdom to earth.

Give us the ability to communicate this truth to others and to call them forth into the destiny You have for them. Not the destiny we think would be best for them.

In the mighty Name of Jesus. Amen

5
Woman and Mother: Mentor and Coach

5
Woman and Mother: Mentor and Coach

THE WOMAN OF VIRTUE FAMOUSLY praised in Proverbs 31 as more resplendent than rubies is a businesswoman.

> *She appraises a field and buys it; from her earnings she plants a vineyard.*
>
> Proverbs 31:16 BSB

> *She makes linen garments and sells them; she delivers sashes to the merchants.*
>
> Proverbs 31:24 BSB

She is also an entrepreneur and an industrious employer who leads by example. Although this woman of virtue is idealised, she nevertheless has some Scriptural counterparts. From the professions mentioned in the writings of the early church, we can see that women were influential across many of the highest strata in society.

Joanna, the wife of Chuza—the steward who managed Herod's estates—financed the itinerant ministry of Jesus and His disciples.[29] Susanna was also a benefactor of His work. (Luke 8:2–3)

Lydia of Thyatira was a wealthy wholesaler of expensive violet fabric—she welcomed Paul and his companions into her home in Philippi. (Acts 16:14–15)

Dorcas was a designer and manufacturer of inner garments and underwear. (Acts 9:39)

Damaris became a believer after hearing Paul preach to the Areopagus, the leading council of statesmen in Athens. (Acts 17:17) The very fact she was present during his address strongly hints at the possibility she was a high-class escort.[30]

Priscilla, along with her husband Aquila, was a tentmaker. (Acts 18:2)

And then there's the deacon Phoebe who was a mentor to Paul.

Err, *mentor*? To *Paul*? Don't choke. Take a deep breath.

The ancient world didn't sideline women or their role in ministry. Sure enough the men were the stars of most Scriptural stories but often women are mentioned, briefly entering various scenes like luminous and spectacular comets. As we have seen in previous chapters, the original text accords women a high status as kingmakers, watchmen, pioneers, bridge-builders, navigators, cupbearers, visionaries, prophets and God-namers—and those roles don't even take into account women like Deborah who were judges, legislators and warriors.

We've been taught—at least I was—that the world of the Scriptures was patriarchal through and through. I've gradually come to doubt that it was. It seems to have been a contrasting patchwork that was increasingly frayed at every seam by cultural tensions: the more the Jewish nation came to be like those around them, the less they valued women.

I believe that many translators are influenced to their deep mind's core with a Greek rationalistic worldview and its attendant animosity towards women. Consequently they have sometimes nuanced their versions in a way that does not truly reflect the original Hebrew with its attendant amity towards women.[31]

Let's take, as just one notable example, the 'woman of virtue' mentioned at the opening of this chapter. Bronwen Speedie reports on teaching about the meaning of this key phrase found in Proverbs 31. She points out:

> *Eshet chayil* is usually translated 'a wife of noble character,' 'a virtuous and capable wife,' 'an excellent wife,' 'a virtuous woman,' or 'a worthy woman.'
>
> These are all positive character traits, but a closer look at the word *chayil* shows that despite it being a common word in the Old Testament, it is *only* in the 3 instances where it is applied to women that translators have considered it to be about sexual purity or industriousness in the home.
>
> *Chayil* is a military term mostly applied to warriors, connoting strength and courage. Some translations and commentators suggest that 'a valiant woman' or 'a woman of valour' is a more accurate translation.[32]

Yes, 'woman of valour' is a much better rendering of this phrase from Proverbs 31 than 'woman of virtue'. It's not that 'woman of virtue' is necessarily wrong. It's that *chayil* is translated inconsistently—and because those variants all occur in the same context they actually become interpretations, rather than translations. They reveal a philosophic stance that is not present in the original text.

The women who are as resplendent as rubies have immense courage and initiative. They are defenders of their household who have been tempered in fire, they are spiritual and domestic champions who are worthy battle-companions for their husbands. They are the armour-bearers, armour-givers and game-changers looked at in the first book in this series.[33] They are in fact paracletes[34] in the struggles of life; they are both gentle doves and protective she-bears.

A similar kind of nuancing and softening has glossed the status of Phoebe in relation to Paul. Many translations of Romans 16:1 describe her as a servant—which is indeed true. However that particular choice of word conceals what other translators reveal: Phoebe was a deacon, an appointment of special status in the early church.[35]

Since some translators consider it impossible for a woman to be a deacon in the light of 1 Timothy 3:8–13, just over half of them translate deacon as *servant* or as *one who is in the ministry of the church*.[36] But only for Phoebe.

The drive to reconcile paradox, remove exceptions, re-order the revolution of Jesus into more comfortable cultural norms means that we try to hide anything that disturbs it. But salvation history is full of paradox, brimming with exceptions, pulsing with revolutions that turn the world upside down and right side up. Is not grace, by nature and definition, all about exception?

The erosion of Phoebe's standing, ensuring that she does not rank with the likes of Paul and Apollos,[37] Stephen, Philip, Procorus, Nicanor, Timon, Parmenas and Nicolas,[38] is a *cultural* tradition still prevalent in our age—it is not Scriptural. Although Phoebe is the only female deacon mentioned in the Bible, she was not the only one in the early church. A letter to the emperor Trajan in around 112 AD refers to two female slaves who were deacons and who were tortured to extract the truth from them. So female deacons weren't necessarily highborn.

Nonetheless it seems likely that Phoebe herself was wealthy and intelligent. Because, besides being a deacon, 'diakonos', she is also described as a 'prostatis'. This is often translated as a helper, friend or assistant—and occasionally as patron or benefactor.[39] However in classical Greek, a person who was referred to as 'prostatis' was a mentor or Olympic coach.[40]

Herbert Lockyer points out that 'prostatis' was a trainer who stood by the athletes to see that they were properly trained and rightly girded when they lined up for the signal. He points out that Handley Moule translated Paul's commendation of Phoebe in Romans 16:2 this way:

> 'She on her part has proved a stand-by (almost a champion, one who stands up for others) of many, aye, and of me among them.'

A champion! A coach, a trainer, an instructor: someone who tutored Paul! Phoebe has gone the extra mile for others. She is truly the woman of valour comparable to the resplendent ruby of Proverbs 31. Lockyer points out she was 'the unselfish, liberal helper or patroness of the saints, conspicuous for her works of charity and also hospitality.'[41]

Now mentoring is not exactly the same as coaching. Mentoring is walking with others but it's not controlling them; it's about guidance, encouragement, being present and listening to the mentee.

In our modern world busyness has become a status people are proud of. 'How are you?' a friend may ask. 'So busy' has become the common response. Mentoring pushes back on our time-poor existence; it's about purposefully investing intentional periods into the lives of others.

Sometimes the greatest gift you can give someone is your time and your presence—being truly there with the person one-on-one, face-to-face in communication. There's so much disconnect in our society that Gen X parents are being begged by their children to put their phones away—and to talk and connect with them!

Coaching,[42] on the other hand, is about deliberate assistance. It's about pushing. We see sports coaches, life coaches and health coaches who help drive and motivate people toward their goals.

Mentoring and coaching have become a very popular buzz words in our vocabulary during recent times. But what does it really mean to have a mentor or to be a mentor in today's world? What is a realistic expectation to have of others and of ourselves?

How do we follow in the footsteps of Phoebe and mentor others as a woman or a wife, as a mother or sister or daughter? How do we bring others into learning, healing and growing without hindering their free will? How can we guide them without stifling their growth journey or gentling the unique challenges and tests God has set before them?

Let's consider the differences between mentors and parents. A mentor is defined by the Webster dictionary as *an experienced and trusted adviser*. According to David Clutterbuck, a mentor is 'a more experienced individual willing to share knowledge with someone less experienced in a relationship of mutual trust.'

If we plan to mentor others we need to be aware of our own motivations and intentions. We should not be fueled by ego or a desire for adulation.

'The mentor essentially helps the learner discover... wisdom.'

Parinita Gupta

The coach, on the other hand, is focused on performance. The mentor is focused on the development of wise and gentle approaches to achieving goals.

'Be wise as serpents and innocent as doves.'

Matthew 10:16 ESV

'Clear is kind. Unclear is unkind.'

Brené Brown

According to researcher Brené Brown, to be kind, we need to be clear in our communication. We need to know what the boundaries and expectations are, otherwise disappointment will win and it can take years or decades to move past it.

Bob Gass tells the story of a youth leader who was fired from his position in a church. The leader said:

> 'After serving the Lord there for two years, I was called into an elders' meeting. They took out a list of all the things I'd done wrong in the past two years. Most of what they said was true, for I was brand new in this work. Then they called for my resignation. What did I learn?
>
> (a) not once did anyone care enough to coach or shepherd me
>
> (b) I'd no idea or warning that I was doing anything wrong
>
> (c) the church leaders never built a relationship with their staff.'[43]

As a young person of 23, I wanted to help others because of my own troubled background and rebelliousness through my early teens, I started my degree in the hope of becoming a youth counsellor. I wanted to be there for other young people just like I had wanted others to be there for me. But, in retrospect, I realise I wanted to rescue others and this, in reality, was always more about me than it ever was about others.

I now recognise my own immaturity at the time I first wanted to mentor others. The opening lecture I attended started with the students on the floor. As we attempted to connect with our inner child, the lecturer said: 'You are here to help others but first you need to get healing yourself.'

I was shocked and disconcerted—there I was determined to learn how to help others and I was startled by this statement that I was the one who needed help! Little did I realise at the time how much brokenness was in my own life that was yet to be healed.

Fast forward sixteen years and I finally qualified as a counselor. But today I am a very different counsellor than I would have been back then, all those years ago. I know now that the tests and refining of the Lord come to purify and redeem the unregenerate parts of our hearts still carrying pride and rebellion.

The healing needs to be a work of God and we need to surrender the idea that it is ever about us and our own power.

It is God who works in and through us. If we think it's about us, we will be tempted to control the means and also manipulate the ending in order to stroke our own ego. Sitting in the space of healing is occupying a position of power since we are working with vulnerable people who can easily be coerced into doing things for approval.

A counselling relationship is both therapeutic and professional, however mentoring can be much more informal. This can mean that boundaries are quite unclear and it is possible, in the power differential, for unholy agendas to emerge.

This is an area we need to be extremely sensitive to as we mentor others or are mentored ourselves.

In the last few years there has been a huge upsurge in conversations about eldership and parenting. Because a spiritual void exists in our family and society, individuals are desperate for guidance and direction. We learn though trial and error, through getting things spectacularly right and disastrously wrong. It's true that we learn through mistakes but, in the process, there can be immense grief and loss. I found that out when I began to understand the gaps and chasms in my own upbringing that had led me down a difficult and lonely path hedged about with much pain and suffering.

So how do we raise mature disciples? That, after all, is what mentoring is really all about—showing others how to follow Jesus and encouraging them on the journey. The stories of the women in this book are guides: through their lives, lessons, mistakes and victories, we can learn what it means to follow Him. We can find in their histories how to mentor others to be kingmakers and cupbearers, sentinels and watchmen, navigators and pioneers, bridge-builders and visionaries, history-makers and culture-changers, princesses and servants.

So let us choose His high calling, never forgetting we cannot achieve anything of lasting value in our own strength—only when we put our hand into the scarred hand of Jesus Himself.

Prayer for myself

LORD, I AM SO DIFFERENT from the virtuous woman so praised in Proverbs. She stepped up and out and was the best she could be. I have been the opposite—sometimes afraid of failure, sometimes afraid *of* success, sometimes afraid *in* success—afraid that others saw through me and I was not what they expected of a successful woman. This locked me into failing, even sometimes when I was succeeding.

I repent of having been less than You made me to be. Forgive me, Heavenly Father, and let my heart come into alignment with Yours as I step up and out for the sake of Your Kingdom.

I am thankful that You have graced me with the ability to live life and live it to the fullest. Forgive me for the many times I have failed to be the best 'me' that I could be and for my lack of gratitude for Your wondrous gifts. Open my eyes and gift me, Lord, with an attitude of gratitude for all You are and all You do. Please write in my heart that You made me to be a woman of valour for the sake of Your Kingdom and give me the grace to live it.

Convict me, Lord, that life is all about You and not about me. I know this in my mind but my heart response is often: 'But what about me?' While that thought remains, however small it is, heaven and earth cannot meet because I am in the way.

Father, I want to mentor others to become their best self. Yet I know this can only happen if I get out of the way. Please be the mentor and allow me to be the vessel through which You work. I am useless until I walk hand in hand with Jesus—the One who came to earth and showed us what You are like. He taught, healed and showed us how to live life to the utmost.

In His name. Amen.

Prayer to bless others

FATHER, AS I TALK and walk with my sisters-in-faith I often hear You say quietly: 'Listen—listen to My words. They are written and inscribed for all time in The Book especially in the first three chapters of Paul's letter to the Ephesians.'

Believe this, my sisters, and live life the way God intended, so that then you are able to say:

I am a saint
Grace and peace are mine
I am blessed with every spiritual blessing
I am chosen before the creation of the world
I am predestined
I am adopted into God's family
I am redeemed
I am forgiven
God's grace is lavished on me
Wisdom and understanding are mine
God's will is made known to me
I am included in Christ
I am sealed with the Holy Spirit
I have a guaranteed inheritance
I am called to hope
I have a glorious inheritance
His incomparably great power works in me
God has given me life
I am seated in heavenly places
I am saved by grace
I am God's workmanship
I am God's masterpiece

I am God's poem
I am brought near through Christ's blood
I am reconciled with others
I have access to the Father
I am a fellow citizen with God's people
I am a dwelling place for God's Spirit
I am a member of the One Body
I share in the promise of Christ
I can approach God with freedom
God is able to do immeasurably more than
I can ask or imagine

What blessings we have and what a blessing we are, as daughters of our Heavenly Father! We are resplendent as rubies. We are His treasure. Truly we are blessed with these unsurpassed riches in order to be a blessing to others.

Thank you, Jesus.

In Your Name—the Name above all names. Amen.

6
Woman: Culture-changer

6
Woman: Culture-changer

CONTEXT IS EVERYTHING. DA CARSON famously said that his father, a Canadian minister, liked to say: 'A text without a *context* is a *pretext* for a proof text.'

I'd heard the following gospel story dozens of times before I realised it was missing a critical piece of context:

> 'He arose and went away to the region of Tyre and Sidon. And He entered a house and did not want anyone to know, yet He could not be hidden. But immediately a woman whose little daughter had an unclean spirit heard of Him and came and fell down at His feet. Now the woman was a Gentile, a Syrophoenician by birth. And she begged Him to cast the demon out of her daughter. And He said to her, "Let the children be fed first, for it is not right to take the children's bread and throw it to the dogs." But she answered Him, "Yes, Lord; yet even the dogs under the table eat the children's crumbs." And He said to her, "For this statement you may go your way; the demon has left your daughter." And she went home and found the child lying in bed and the demon gone.'
>
> Mark 7:24–30 ESV

Matthew's story is very similar but adds some pertinent details:

> *Jesus went away from there, and withdrew into the district of Tyre and Sidon. And a Canaanite woman from that region came out and began to cry out, saying, "Have mercy on me, Lord, Son of David; my daughter is cruelly demon-possessed." But He did not answer her a word. And His disciples came and implored Him, saying, "Send her away, because she keeps shouting at us." But He answered and said, "I was sent only to the lost sheep of the house of Israel." But she came and began to bow down before Him, saying, "Lord, help me!" And He answered and said, "It is not good to take the children's bread and throw it to the dogs." But she said, "Yes, Lord; but even the dogs feed on the crumbs which fall from their masters' table." Then Jesus said to her, "O woman, your faith is great; it shall be done for you as you wish." And her daughter was healed at once.'*

Matthew 15:21 NASB

In Matthew's account, Jesus is almost callous in His reaction to the woman. '*I was sent only to the lost sheep of the house of Israel*,' He says. '*It is not good to take the children's bread and throw it to the dogs.*'

Huh? Like what? Did we miss something? Is this the same Jesus we thought we knew? Is this the Jesus who talked to a Samaritan woman? Who cast out demons all through the Gentile towns of the Decapolis? Who has no issue with healing a Roman centurion's servant? What's this sudden high-and-mighty uppity bit about healing being reserved for the Jews? Why are there boundaries and shut-downs in place that have never been there before?

Now a lot of commentators tie themselves inside out trying to explain away these words. They want to soften the contempt and moderate the harsh indifference. There appears, on the surface, to be grand scale racial prejudice in the words of Jesus. But what would

He have against a Syrophoenician woman? After all, there's one in His bloodline. And not just any Phoenician woman either—but the 'bad' girl to end all 'bad' girls! Jezebel herself.

Yes, the ancestry of Jesus includes Jezebel through her daughter Athaliah who was married to Joram, king of Judah. She was the grandmother of Joash, the sole heir who survived her murderous purge of the royal family when her son, Ahaziah, died. Ultimately she was the great-great-grandmother of Uzziah mentioned in the genealogy of Jesus.

There's also a few Canaanite women in His bloodline—Tamar, the mother of Perez, as well as Rahab, the mother of Boaz. In addition, there's the wife of Boaz—the Moabite woman, Ruth. These three women are specifically mentioned by Matthew. The only other one in the list is Bathsheba. However she is not recorded by name; she is down as 'Uriah's wife'. Perhaps this is a subtle hint that Bathsheba, like her first husband Uriah, was a Hittite. After all the genealogy otherwise lists only foreign women and, most peculiarly, names like Sarah, Rebecca and Leah are missing.

Jesus would have known the role of foreign women was incredibly significant: in the days of Elijah, a widow from the Syrophoenician town of Zarephath, was called by God to preserve the prophet's life. So why did He act the way He did towards this particular Syrophoenician woman?

At the beginning I said that some important context is missing. It's this: the woman was not simply Syrophoenician, she was not simply Canaanite, she was also *Greek*. Many translators call her a Gentile—quite true—but the original text of Mark 7:26 clearly specifies her background as Greek.

'So what?' you might think. 'What difference does that make?'

A lot, as it happens. To call any Greek person of those days 'a dog' wasn't necessarily insulting. It was nothing more than saying they ascribed to a particular philosophy: the school of thought known as 'the dog-like'.

We call them the Cynics.

> *Cynics don't learn anything. Because cynicism is a self-imposed blindness; a rejection of the world because we are afraid it will hurt us or disappoint us. Cynics always say 'no.' But saying 'yes' begins things. Saying 'yes' is how we grow.*
>
> Stephen Colbert

Over time, we've developed attitudes about cynicism that don't accurately reflect the philosophy of the past. It wasn't nearly as anti-hope or anti-faith as modern cynicism has become. Nevertheless the seeds were there: the Greek Cynics are seen as the originators of the ideal of anarchy; they held low views of those in authority and were shameless in their public behaviour.[44]

The description of the woman's attitude and behaviour subtly hints she was indeed a Cynic. She hounded and shouted at Jesus and the disciples—an action that would have been seen as shameless and disrespectful of authority.

The Cambridge Dictionary describes cynical people of today as those who believe others are motivated purely by self-interest; cynics are distrustful of human sincerity or integrity. They are concerned only with their own interests and typically disregard accepted standards in order to achieve them.[45]

So, Jesus in being confronted by a cynic is also facing someone who is so lacking in faith in *anyone*—let alone Himself as the Son of the Most High—that what she wants is impossible.

Faith—even as small as a mustard seed—is what He asks us to bring to Him so He can present it to the Father, uniting our faith with His as He mediates on our behalf for a miracle. It was a spectacular lack of faith—utter unbelief—that meant the people of His own hometown, Nazareth, received so little of the miraculous:

> *Jesus said to them, 'A prophet is not without honour except in his own town, among his relatives and in his own home.' He could not do any miracles there, except lay His hands on a few sick people and heal them. He was amazed at their lack of faith.*
>
> Mark 6:4–6 NIV

Pure, unadulterated cynicism is in total opposition to the faith and trust necessary for answered prayer. And that's what Jesus is challenging head-on by His words to the Syrophoenician woman. Unless there's a spark of faith in her, He could speak words of healing and they would wither immediately. She'd return home to find no change in her daughter and her cynicism would be immeasurably reinforced. In fact, she'd probably be out uprooting the tiny shoots of faith in her neighbours who had heard of Jesus the wonder-worker.

So to say anything would be, as Jesus mentioned on another occasion, like casting pearls before swine. A cynic distrusts and disparages the motives of others, shows contempt for honesty and morality, is pessimistic, bitter and sneering and often exploits others' scruples of others.

This is not the kind of person you waste faith on. It's possibly even counterproductive.

> *The cynic thinks that he is being practical and that the hopeful person is not. It is actually the other way around. Cynicism is paralyzing, while the naïve person tries what the cynic says is impossible and sometimes succeeds.*
>
> Charles Eisenstein

When the disciples have had enough of being harassed, they beg

Jesus to send her away. But Jesus doesn't. At last, He breaks His silence and begins to speak to the woman. And perhaps in His own behaviour with its hints of contempt, subtle disparagement and silent disregard for her as a person, He's holding a mirror up to her own soul.

'It is not good to take the children's bread and throw it to the dogs,' He says.

Now's her opening. Even the tiniest crumb of faith will make the difference and perhaps she knows it. *'Yes, Lord; but even the dogs feed on the crumbs which fall from their masters' table.'*

It's witty, rather than contemptuous. It's whimsical, rather than bitter. It's clever, rather than disparaging.

Her persistence has paid off. *'O woman, your faith is great; it shall be done for you as you wish,'* Jesus says.

Her encounter with Jesus has apparently changed her. He describes her faith as 'great'—desperation for her daughter has turned her world upside down. Perhaps she's about to become a very different kind of *dog*—one like Caleb, the great Jewish hero whose name has a double meaning: *dog* and *whole-hearted*.

As her own heart heals, she has the opportunity to change the culture around her. So it can be for us. We can be part of a dysfunctional family system or toxic work environment that breeds cynicism. We can absorb the mocking, sarcastic atmosphere so regularly that we're unaware we've been imbibing unbelief. We can resort to derision and ridicule as a coping mechanism to enable us to mentally handle the tension of the environment. We can criticise without being constructive.

If we're in that situation and have found, like the Syrophoenician woman, that God is silent then follow her example. Be persistent. Let desperation drive you to Jesus, not away from Him.

Because, like her, we're called to be culture-changers. To become whole-hearted and then to point the way for others to do likewise.

Prayer for myself:

ABBA, TODAY I COME before you and I repent and ask for your forgiveness for my mistrust and distrust of You and others. I have not known and understood what love-bonds are and I have been attached to others through fear-bonds.

Where my heart and spirit have been wounded and there has been a lack of love and affection, please remove my pain and place Your tender love into their very depths. I want to be attached to You, not to fear. Where I have been attached in unhealthy ways to people, events and places, I ask You to unattach me.

Where those bonds have led me into cynicism, I ask You to remove the bitterness, resentment and pain that has caused me to self-protect and become skeptical of faith—and of Your promises to respond to faith.

I know that this has been my response to lack and loss. I've pushed others away with cruel words before they could be close enough to hurt me again. Forgive me for the times my actions have hurt others. Forgive me for believing lies and for making vows to myself about never trusting others or deciding that everyone is only interested in self. I renounce the lie that others are only interested in themselves and that there is always a scheming agenda behind kindness and love.

Abba, forgive me for the times I've allowed hope to be crushed even when I've seen the compassion and generosity of others. I ask You today to comfort me and be my source of strength and peace. Show me how to lean into You and Your way.

My way is not working anymore so I ask that You forgive me for using cynicism and sarcasm as a false refuge and a shield from pain, instead of running to You. I renounce cynicism and I ask Jesus to empower my resolve to seek You and Your kingdom in faith.

I choose You today, I ask that You bless me and pour Your healing balm into the empty places of my heart. Surround my spirit with the peace that is like a river running from beneath Your throne.

I thank You that You are enough for me today and every day. I thank You that, through being hidden in You, I am enough today. I am grateful for Your blessings in my life.

Cynicism has been the lens that has tainted the way I see the world and others people. I want to put your glasses on, Abba, and see others and the world as you see them.

I want to see them through heaven's eyes.

In the Name of Jesus. Amen.

Prayer to bless others:

FATHER GOD, You are the Life within all life in others as well as me. Give us, Father give us eyes to see Your image in the very depths of the 'other's' being—to see that, just like me, the 'other' is made in Your image and likeness at the core of their being. This should strip away all disrespect, dishonour and distrust. Replace these, Lord with respect, honour and trust. Increase our awareness that there are no strangers in this world but only friends that we have not met yet.

Make us all aware, Lord, that we are often the only signpost of Your Kingdom in this beautiful and wonderful world that many will see this week.

Father, You gave us stewardship of this beautiful and life-sustaining world that You created. Teach us, Father, of the connectedness between relationship with You, relationship with Your creation and relationship with each other. Grant us the gift of repentance and forgive us for our neglect of Your world and our personal relationships. Teach us that when we repent of wrongdoing, we do not try to be a different person, but rather we turn to and become our true self made in Your image—the image of a sinless God.

Open our eyes Lord to the beauty that is all around us. Grant us the ability to see beyond the obvious to the very heart of life—to You, as you hide us in the cleft of the rock. Be our first and only refuge, Lord. Wrap us in Your mantle of protection and hide us from all that is not of you. Keep us safe and may we confess that You are the Way, the Truth and the Life and we pray in the name of Jesus, who came that we might have life and have it in abundance.

7
Woman and Mother: Princess

7
Woman and Mother: Princess

WE'VE LOOKED AT THE ROLES of various women in the biblical record and seen the quiet significance of their actions—and how they've so often been heralds of momentous turning points in history. So it's probably time to sound a note of caution.

What happened to change the place of women from one of great esteem to one of such unimportance that even their names are unknown? At the beginning of the book of Exodus, we know the names of four of the five women who were instrumental in saving the lives of Moses. At the end of the book of Numbers, we know the names of the five women who successfully petitioned Moses to inherit land in their own right.[46]

And as the book of Judges opens, we hear the stories of Deborah and Jael—and during this same period of time, we also have the detailed romance of the book of Ruth and the actual words of Hannah's prophetic song. However as the era of the Judges marches on towards the time of the Kings, we begin to see signs of the shift. The names of women are starting to become obscured: it's Jephthah's *daughter*, the Levite's *concubine*, Samson's first *wife*.

By the time the monarchy is well-established, only royal women are identified—and not always then. Jeroboam's wife plays a significant role in approaching the prophet Ahijah on behalf of her son, crown prince Abijah, but we never learn her name. History only records that of the males in that particular story.

What a contrast to the age of the Exodus when the only name we *don't* know is that of Pharaoh's daughter—and it may well be concealed simply to ensure the Pharaoh himself cannot be identified. After all, no worse fate could befall an Egyptian ruler than to have his name erased from history. Well, maybe a worse fate could befall him—his name being forgotten while those of two ordinary midwives are remembered!

It seems that, as men began to take for themselves thrones and platforms, pedestals and podiums, women were increasingly relegated to an inferior position. It's earthly kingship—the desire for power, position and authority that rightfully belongs only to God—that's the critical issue when it comes to the status of women in Scripture.

Jesus, the one true King of kings, began the restoration of women as He appointed them kingmakers and benefactors, cupbearers and watchmen, innovators and navigators.

When we are adopted into the family of God, we become His sisters: princesses of the realm of heaven. So, let's take care. Let's show grace. Let's return honour for dishonour and blessing for exploitation; let's learn from the mistakes of the kings and the patriarchs and not repeat them.

Instead of coveting the platforms and podiums men have created for themselves in today's sacred and secular cultures, and instead of reproducing their error in usurping the throne of God, let's simply step into the roles He calls us to fulfil. Let's stop being anxious that we've been marginalised and ignored. God pursues us out in the margins, sends His angels to meet us in the wilderness, promises to bind up our wounds and relieve our heartache and oppression.

Most of all, let's take Jesus as our role model. Let's seek first the Kingdom of God and His righteousness and not secretly crave those platforms of power and influence in our world. For far too many of the men on those platforms do not end well—either Scripturally or in the modern day.

Let's hold instead the scarred hand of Jesus and keep our eyes on Him, not on the pedestal. Let's direct the gaze of others to Him on His throne, not to ourselves. Or even to the projected images of ourselves that we might glue firmly into the pages of Scripture.

With this thought in mind—that it's easy to see ourselves in the lives of biblical characters and excuse our actions on that basis—let's look at two princesses.

The first is Gladys—and her name actually means *princess*.

Most likely you've never heard of her. And to be honest, we can't be a hundred percent certain she's actually in the pages of Scripture—however, the weight of historical evidence tends towards it being far more likely than not.

Gladys was a British princess of the first century; her father was the tribal chieftain Caradog who was renowned as a fierce and unrelenting opponent of Roman expansionism into Britain. For nine years he defied the empire's legions, emerging victorious on each occasion. But the tide eventually turned against him. Escaping capture in his final battle, he fled to his mother-in-law, hoping she'd help him rebuild his resistance forces. Instead she handed him over to the Romans.

Along with his family Caradog was taken to Rome. It was expected he'd be the centerpiece of the usual victory parade to be followed by humiliation and public execution. But the Emperor Claudius and the Roman Senate were curious about this famous blue-painted barbarian whom they called 'Caractacus'. They wanted to see for themselves the savage who had resisted the might of the legions for longer than any other warrior general.

Now apparently Caractacus had acquired an insight over the years that was to stand him in good stead: he had learned how his enemies thought. Indeed, his understanding of the Roman mind was exceptional. So when he was given an opportunity to speak, he made an eloquent appeal. He struck at their weakness: the lingering desire of the old patrician families to create a noble legacy. Rome, he said, had a chance to create an everlasting memorial which would enhance the glory of the empire. And it was only by choosing mercy towards a defeated enemy that this could be achieved.

Bravo and 'thumbs up' was the reaction.

Yes, the Senate decided to allow Caractacus and his family to live. But of course they could not be allowed to return to Britain to foster rebellion once more. Instead they were sentenced to be kept under house arrest in Rome itself for seven years. Although 'house arrest' meant Caractacus would have been chained between some warders—most likely the elite Praetorian guard—it was a relatively comfortable set-up with visitors allowed.

Now it turned out that the Emperor Claudius was so taken by the beauty and charm of the lovely princess Gladys that he eventually adopted her. Perhaps it helped that the Latin form of 'Gladys' was 'Claudia'.

Claudia's beauty came to be celebrated in the verses of the poet Martial. She married a Roman senator named Rufus Pudens and had a son named Linus.

> 'Do your best to get here before winter. Eubulus greets you, and so do Pudens, Linus, Claudia...'

2 Timothy 4:21 NIV

Some people think that those last three names in this second last verse of what is widely accepted as Paul's final epistle are just a coincidence. That it's impossible that a British princess could possibly be named here. It seems to me this is a reaction to the elaborate legends that have grown up about the spread of Christianity in first century Britain.

Paul was under house arrest in Rome for two years; Caractacus was under house arrest for seven. It's far from impossible that they knew each other. Sifting through 'history' and winnowing out the 'legend' is extremely difficult, given some of these exaggerations.

So let's not claim too much but let's not claim too little either. Let's not accept blindly, nor dismiss out of hand. *Let's be discerning*.

God calls everyone—the great and the small. He calls the young and the old, the privileged and the oppressed, the wise and the foolish, the princess and the beggar.

Let's be discerning. I know I wrote that same sentence only a paragraph back but the reason I repeat this is because I don't want you to default to any preconceived notions when it comes to another princess—this time one who unquestionably appears in Scripture. Let me preface her introduction with the following thought: because Scripture records the history of different heroes of the faith, generally without comment, there's a tendency to think God approves of what they did.

We have to be careful not to exalt people onto the throne that rightfully belongs to God alone.

The second princess I'd like us to consider is the one after whom Israel is named. That statement may come as quite a surprise if you thought the nation of Israel came from the renaming of Jacob by the angel he wrestled with at the ford of Jabbok. Of course, that's true but still the name bestowed by the angel didn't spring out of nowhere. It's ultimately derived from the name of a woman.

Jacob's name, *the one who grasps the heel*, is similar in meaning to that of his mother Rebecca, *a snare for the foot*. However, Israel is basically the male version of his grandmother's name. Israel, *prince with God*. Sarah, *princess with God*.

Sarah was the wife of Abraham.

One statement tends to colour so many people's views of her. It is God's command to Abraham: '*Do whatever Sarah tells you.*' (Genesis 21:12 NLT)

Sarah had becoming intent on ensuring Isaac would inherit everything his father owned. The incident that provoked her was Hagar's son—Abraham's firstborn, Ishmael—laughing at Isaac during the party where he was weaned. Many versions say Ishmael 'mocked' Isaac but that's a biased interpretation. Elsewhere the Hebrew word translated *mocked* is simply *laughed*. It is the same word used to describe Sarah's reaction when she heard God say she would have a son. It is the same word used to create Isaac's name: *he laughs*.

This is not to say that Ishmael didn't ridicule Isaac; it is simply to say that, if he did, then Sarah did the same to God. God rebuked her and forgave her; but she could not pass the forgiveness on. She did not learn from what she experienced.

In fact, that's the nature of Sarah's character. Throughout her life there were incidents that eerily echo the situation she forced onto Hagar—but she never learned from them. When Abraham went to Gerar, he convinced Sarah to say she was his sister, not his wife. As a result, she was taken into Abimelech's harem. A stranger in a foreign country, pregnant for the first time, surrounded by women who were suddenly and inexplicably barren and thus probably insanely jealous of her fertility, she was abandoned by the husband who should have been her primary protector.

These are the very same things Hagar experienced fourteen years previously, with serious abuse thrown in. Sarah reaped what she sowed. But did she learn compassion from the experience?

It's doubtful. When Hagar was finally sent away, it was with nothing but some food and water. Abraham was an immensely rich man—staggering wealth was piled on him by Pharaoh and Abimelech despite his deception—but he didn't give even a donkey as a gift or provide an escort for safety when his son was exiled by the woman who engineered his existence.

Sarah was harsh; Abraham did her bidding because God told him to—but that begs some questions. Why did God allow Hagar to be sent off like this? Why did He tell her to return and submit to Sarah's abuse when she'd run away years before?

The answers, I believe, are about harm minimisation.

How could Hagar have survived, alone and pregnant in the wilderness, with all the dangers she would have encountered? She could have given birth while scouting daily for food and water but it would have been a perilous undertaking.

Later, when God told Abraham to do as Sarah said, it's not necessarily because she's right. I believe it's because she's become vindictive. She's been in the same situation as Hagar but not learned compassion; she's been in the same situation as Ishmael but not learned forgiveness. She's been complicit with her husband in deceiving two rulers and receiving extraordinary lavish gifts when they become 'unwelcome' and were sent away. Yet when her surrogate son and his mother become 'unwelcome' to her, she makes sure they are sent away with far, far, far less than an honoured overnight guest would receive.

None of this 'do unto others as you would have them do unto you' notion. Sarah is entitled. Her 'princess' status meant privilege. And her story is one of grace received but not of grace regifted.

God, in my view, therefore minimised the harm to Hagar and Ishmael by telling Abraham to do what Sarah wanted and send them away.

Let us therefore not model ourselves on Sarah—as we're sometimes exhorted to do. Let us look instead to Jesus:

> *We do not have a high priest who cannot sympathise with our weaknesses, but One who has been tempted in all things as we are, yet without sin. Therefore let us draw near with confidence to the throne of grace, so that we may receive mercy and find grace to help in time of need.*
>
> Hebrews 4:15–16 NAS

God has appointed us, His princesses, to be grace-givers. The oldest meaning of 'lady' is *bread-giver*. In a spiritual sense, that means to be one who dispenses the Word of God, the knowledge of Jesus, the Bread of Life.

There's a remarkable comment that Jesus once made about the Bread of Life. The implications are shattering. In response to the people's request for a sign from heaven—on the day immediately following the miracle of the loaves and fishes—He said:

> *'Very truly I tell you, it is not Moses who has given you the bread from heaven, but it is My Father who gives you the true bread from heaven.'*
>
> John 6:32 NIV

Now this comment is not remarkable for what it says, it's remarkable that it needed to be said at all! It's gob-smackingly incredible that these people were so scrupulous in their religious views they remained suspicious of Jesus' claims, yet they had to be reminded that *Moses was not God*. The words of Jesus tell us that the miraculous works of God were being attributed to Moses!

Now you might think this is an exceptional case. But it's not.

Just as the people of the first century lifted Moses to the throne of heaven, so too we have a tendency to overlook the flaws of our culture heroes. It doesn't matter whether those heroes are celebrity Christians or Scriptural champions.

We need to be discerning. Because far too much damage occurs when we allow forgiveness of abuse to become defence of abuse. We batter wounds rather than bind them up when we substitute our human idols for Jesus. He's the gold standard, no one else.

God calls us to be His princesses.

Let's not forget, however, how we ended the first chapter in this book: throw down your crown and bow before Him, gifting Him all of yourself. No matter what your past, don't let it define you. Don't let abuse or rebellion, shame or stupidity, fear or frailty, or even your own sense of unworthiness hold you back. Accept His incomparable invitation. If He calls you to be a kingmaker, like Mary of Bethany or the woman of the well in Samaria, don't think you're disqualified! If He calls you to be a visionary like Hagar, a navigator like Hannah, a bridge-builder like Leah, a sentinel like Mary or a mentor like Phoebe, then don't think you're disqualified either!

There's an old saying but a true one: *God doesn't call the qualified, He qualifies the called.*

Believe in His call.

Prayer for myself:

FATHER, FEAR HAS SO OFTEN held me back from becoming my best self—the person You want me to be. I heard Your call to step up and to step out. I heard Your still, small voice asking me to be a kingdom-builder in new and wonderful ways. I heard You say my name and ask me to help build a bridge connecting heaven and earth.

But I was afraid to say 'Yes' to Your call.

What was I afraid of? Was it fear of what others would think? Yes. Was it fear of failure? Yes, that too. Was it, paradoxically, fear of success? Yes.

Yes. I admit these fears and so many others. I see them so clearly at last and I repent.

I am sorry that I failed to do the good I could have done if only I had slipped my hand into Yours. I am sorry that I have not lived with confidence in Your promises or walked with You, hand in hand into the future.

It's said that fear is faith in evil that hasn't happened yet. Forgive me, Father for having faith in evil and not in You. Grant me the grace to accept Your forgiveness and, whatever the turmoil in my life, to put my faith in You and the Man who stilled the storm on the waters of the Sea of Galilee.

Amen.

Prayer to bless others:

I PRAY WITH AND FOR MY SISTERS—Father, You created us in Your image to be princesses of integrity, respect, honour and faith. Father, give us the desire and passion to create an intentional culture of honour so that it will be on earth as it is with You in heaven. And so let heaven and earth meet with a kiss of love that comes only from doing Your will. Teach every one of us that when we honour one another we also honour You. And when we fail to honour our sisters and brothers, we fail to honour You. When I fail to honour myself, I also fail to honour You. Teach us all, Father, that honour and courtesy is the hallmark of Your Kingdom.

Teach us also, Father, that Your word is a light to our feet. When we follow You closely, walking in Your footsteps along the paths You have laid out for us, then we are protected from all that is not of You. Let us see with clarity that we can only become the best we can be—whatever that may be—if we are women who respect and honour You, and respect and honour others along with ourselves as well.

Brood over my sisters, Lord. Holy Spirit, surround them with Your love and Your presence. Kindle in them the fire of Your glory and honour.

Father, Jesus, Holy Spirit, be the centre—be the ever-present still point of our turning world.

Give us all the ability to shine Your light in a dark world. And to be salt in a society that has lost its savour, along with the understanding of what it means to endure—despite the hardships we encounter. We praise and thank You for being our hope and our inspiration.

In Jesus' Name. Amen.

Endnotes

1. To hear this anthem in all its polyphonic majesty, you may like to listen to Patrick Dupré Quigley conducting *Seraphic Fire and the Sebastians* as they perform GF Handel's *Zadok the Priest* from his *Coronation Anthems* on YouTube (www.youtube.com/watch?v=8e9X4WSCTUk) or Riga Cathedral School Choir (www.youtube.com/watch?v=w5A24zD27MQ)

2. The definition of a kingmaker is: *a person or group that has great influence on a royal or political succession, without themselves being a viable candidate.* Kingmakers may use political, monetary, religious, and military means to influence the succession. (Wikipedia) Certainly this is true for Nathan and Zadok who, at the behest of Bathsheba, ensured the young prince Solomon was made king, rather than his half-brother Adonijah.

3. The placement of his account—between the scheming of Caiaphas and the visit by Judas to the chief priests— gives the impression it was two days before the Passover, but this assumes a chronological order rather than a thematic one. Matthew has not locked any specific timing down here in the way John has done.

4. Although Luke's account is the most detailed, it does leave

out a critical point mentioned by both Matthew and Mark: Jesus was anointed on the *head* as well as the *feet*. The Jewish audience Matthew and Mark were writing for would have understood both the spiritual and political significance of Mary pouring oil on Jesus' head: Simon Peter might have been the herald who proclaimed the Messiah in *word* but Mary was the herald who proclaimed the Messiah in *deed*. However the cultural nuances of anointing—speaking to the Jews of the appointment of priests and kings—didn't carry across into any Gentile understanding of the ceremony. It seems to me the most likely reason Luke glossed over the oil on the head and instead pointed out that Mary kissed Jesus' feet was because he had a Gentile readership in mind. *Kissing the feet* said 'king' to non-Jews, *anointing* said 'king' to Jews. However note the immense cultural chasm: *kissing the feet* is obeisance; it is a subservient action. *Anointing* on the other hand is the act of a social peer raising another up to a higher position. In miniature, this illustrates the tension between Hebrew and Greek thinking: submission to the Greeks was *putting another down*; submission to the Hebrews was *lifting another up*. See *God's Panoply: The Armour of God and the Kiss of Heaven* for further detail on how this impacts Paul's (in)famous words: 'Wives, submit to your husbands.'

5   This may not mean she was weeping copiously all over Him. It's far more likely that, along with breaking open her alabaster jar of fragrant spikenard scented with myrrh, she also broke open one of her tear bottles. These bottles full of tears were usually kept so that a woman could show appropriate grief and respect for the dead at a funeral by a significant show of weeping. Psalm 56:8 NLT says: '*You keep track of all my sorrows. You have collected all my tears in Your bottle. You have recorded each one in Your book.*' This reference to a tear bottle is not a metaphor; such slim glass bottles actually existed.

6   So many questions are raised in my mind by the fact Simon let this historic opportunity pass by. Now in no way do I intend to denigrate the contribution of Mary of Bethany to salvation history, but I have to ask: was God's first choice for kingmaker a disabled man? A ritually unclean bigot crippled with leprosy? Or, to give him the benefit of the doubt, perhaps simply a man who, while being deeply drawn to Jesus, was too insecure within himself and so conscious of his own religious impurity that he did not dare touch the One he considered to be a prophet. Perhaps he held back from the customary welcome of kiss, water and oil because of a possible rebuff he could not bring himself to face.

Simon's story, of course, brings us face-to-face with our own perception of our inadequacies. Do we sometimes hold back from what God wants of us because we're too conscious of our own disability and damage? When we focus on ourselves—or give in to the fear of what others might think of us—instead of looking towards God's enabling power, we will always be reticent, hesitant, stand-offish. Simon lost his chance. But when I think about it, so did Lazarus, so did the other disciples. Isn't that so often the way with us too? When the disciples saw the host refrain from the traditional welcome, each of them had a choice. It would have been easy to find water to wash Jesus' feet. But they didn't.

I am reminded of Hannah, featured later in this book. She was God's navigator, introducing a change in direction during the time when the high priest was negligent and his sons corrupt. Mary was also God's navigator for her time because, similarly, the Jewish priesthood of the first century had become corrupt.

My prayer for each reader of this book is that you will have the courage when God sends opportunities your way to take what He offers and not, for fear of rebuff or rejection, stand back and let others take them.

7 Beersheba can also mean *well of the seven*, which may refer to the seven ewe lambs that Abraham gave Abimelech as witness to the oath.

8 The Hebrew word 'beer' describes both a *well* and a *pit*. The first two times it is used in Scripture it describes tar pits, the third time occurs in the story of Hagar's flight from Sarah and is the first time it is used connected with water.

9 Clootie means *little cloth*. A clootie well one of the many varieties of sacred well across northern Europe that include healing wells, holy wells, wishing wells, pin wells and lady wells. The practice of dressing wells with ribbons and flowers seems to be an innovation of recent centuries but the veneration of wells has a long history. The tradition of associating them predominately with women goes back even further.

10 In the folklore of Ireland, the motif of the sacred well is bound up with kingship. One such tale is told of Niall Noighiallach. He and his four brothers went hunting, and found themselves astray in the wilderness where they stopped to cook part of the game they had killed. Each in turn went off to look for water and came upon a well guarded by a hideous crone who would give water only in return for a kiss. Three of the brothers refused outright, Fiachra granted her a fleeting kiss, while Niall not only kissed her but consented to sleep with her as well. Immediately she was transformed into a young girl more radiantly beautiful than the sun. She was, she explained, the sovereignty of Ireland and she foretold that Niall and his descendants would hold unbroken rule, apart from two kings of the posterity of Fiachra who were foretokened by his brief kiss.

11   http://www.orkneyjar.com/tradition/sacredwater/index.html (1 March 2019)

12   Actually God does not call Himself 'Yahweh', which means *He is who He is*, in the account of the burning bush where He reveals His name to Moses. He in fact calls Himself, 'Ehyeh', *I am who I am and I will be who I will be.*

13   Strictly speaking at this time in the story, Abraham is still 'Abram'. He hasn't yet raised a name covenant with God and received a new name. Nor has Sarai, who will later be known as Sarah. However, to simplify this chapter for readers, I will consistently use Abraham and Sarah, even when 'Abram' and 'Sarai' would be more strictly accurate.

14   That's extraordinary in itself, but even more extraordinary is this: in her native land, Egypt, her name is connected with the ruins of a temple to the goddess Isis. Through her residence with Abraham and Sarah, she comes to know the living God.

15   Genesis 21:14–20.

16   They were supported in the battle for the Holy Land by British yeomanry and New Zealand troopers; Pacific Islanders who sailed up the coast, keeping valuable supply lines open; by Sikh, Nepalese and Indian battalions, and by Arab irregulars under the command of TE Lawrence, otherwise known as 'Lawrence of Arabia'.

17   1 Kings 11:19.

18   Some English translations use the word '*praise*' in the biblical text before Leah makes her comment on the birth of Judah. These, however, should more correctly be '*blessed*'.

19   I conclude that Belial was actually a fallen angelic power

rather than some abstract quality of *worthlessness* (which is how many translations render the phrase '*sons of Belial*') because of the words of Paul in 2 Corinthians 6:15 NIV, '*What harmony is there between Christ and Belial?*' In this verse Paul is clearly contrasting Christ with a demonic power, so I am taking that particular lead and choosing to consider it that way throughout Scripture.

20 The first time the phrase Yahweh Sabaoth is used is to describe the tabernacle at Shiloh in 1 Samuel 1:3. However, Hannah is the first person recorded as using it.

21 The count of 20 generations assumes that the genealogy actually lists every generation (as shown below). This is by no means certain. It is difficult to know, for example, if Izhar the grandson of Levi is the same man as Amminadab. Both have a son named Korah and similarly named descendents, suggesting they are the same person, though one may simply be father to the other. In addition, from 1 Chronicles 6:22–25, it appears that about seven generations back from Samuel there may have been intermarriage by distant cousins, making a possible alternative count of 14 generations back to Levi. However, this count again assumes the genealogy contains no gaps.

Samuel → Elkanah → Jeroham → Eliel|Eliab → Toah|Nahath →Zuph|Zophai → Elkanah → Mahath|Ahimoth → Amasai → Elkanah → Joel → Azarah → Zephaniah → Tahath → Assir → Ebiasaph → Korah → Izhar|Amminadab → Kohath → Levi

22 *'My soul glorifies the Lord*
and my spirit rejoices in God my Saviour,
for He has been mindful
of the humble state of his servant.

From now on all generations will call me blessed,

for the Mighty One has done great things for me—
holy is His name.

His mercy extends to those who fear Him,
from generation to generation.

He has performed mighty deeds with His arm;
He has scattered those who are proud in their inmost thoughts.

He has brought down rulers from their thrones
but has lifted up the humble.

He has filled the hungry with good things
but has sent the rich away empty.

He has helped His servant Israel,
remembering to be merciful
to Abraham and his descendants forever,
just as He promised our ancestors.'

Luke 1:46–55 NIV

23   A messiah has been referred to before, but not the 'Lord's Messiah'. According to Linda Campbell, Hannah is also the first to describe herself as a 'handmaid' in relation to God. However, it seems to me that, in at least one of the five times she uses the term 'handmaid' or 'maidservant' in the first chapter of 1 Samuel, she is describing herself in relation to Eli. Still she does use the term 'handmaid' in reference to God three times in 1 Samuel 1:11 alone (although this is not clear in all translations.)

24   Or 'shokeling'. See https://www.youtube.com/watch?v=vdkxTire4X8 for historical footage of Jewish people praying this way at the Western Wall in the early twentieth century. Make sure you watch through to the end of the one-minute clip.

25 Rosh Hashanah.

26 'Better the life in hand than dwelling on lives unlived', http://debbielustig.blogspot.com/ (accessed 27 September 2019)

27 See en.wikipedia.org/wiki/New_Testament_people_named_Mary. These include: Mary, the mother of Jesus; Mary the Magdalene; Mary of Bethany (who is almost certainly, at least in my view, the same person as the Magdalene); Mary the mother of James and Joses, who is probably the same Mary who is described as just the mother of James; Mary the mother of John Mark; Mary who may also be called Salome; Mary of Clopas and the 'other' Mary.

28 John 19:25.

29 Since the Hebrew name 'Joanna' is widely regarded as the same as the Roman name 'Junia', Joanna may in fact be referred to in Romans 16:7 as a fellow Jew who had been in prison with Paul and Andronicus. Since the term for 'fellow Jews' is ambiguous, meaning both *kinsmen* and *countrymen*, it is possible Junia was actually related to Paul, not simply the same nationality. In Romans 16:7, Paul describes Junia as '*distinguished among the apostles*' which, back in those days, meant that she would have had to have known Jesus in the flesh. As a financial supporter of the ministry of Jesus, Joanna would certainly have qualified in that regard. See www.theologyofwork.org/key-topics/women-workers-in-the-new-testament (accessed 22 November 2019)

30 The 'hetairai', *companions*, were high-class escorts renowned for their intellectual prowess. Men engaging these courtesans' services desired stimulating debate as well as sex. See theologyofwork.org/key-topics/women-workers-in-the-new-testament (accessed 22 November 2019)

31 See several important examples outlined in *More Precious than Pearls*, the first book in this series, which explores a Jewish rabbinical understanding of the significant role of women during the time of the Exodus—a role that has been completely obscured in modern English translations.

32 This particular quote comes from godsdesignperth.org/2018/08/09/christian-conferences-and-the-danger-of-a-single-story/ (accessed 23 November 2019), however it is worth looking at many of Bronwen's fine articles on *eshet chayil*.

33 Also looked at more comprehensively in *God's Panoply: The Armour of God and the Kiss of Heaven*, Armour Books.

34 The word 'paraclete' is often translated in English as *comforter* or *advocate*. However, it has two separate meanings in Greek, depending on its context. Literally *'the one who stands beside'*, it has a legal sense as well as a military sense. In the legal sense, it is like a counsellor in a courtroom who advises and advocates on your behalf. In a military sense, it is the person who has trained with you as your battle companion and who, in the thickest fighting, will turn back to back with you so you are protected from behind. If you fall, your paraclete will move to stand over you and defend you, and will also after the battle take you off the field, tend to your wounds and comfort you while injured.

35 Paul mentions thirty people or households in Romans 16, sending greetings or making commendations. Phoebe is the first of these and seems, by her pre-eminence as well as the request Paul makes on her behalf, to be his ambassador and the bearer of his epistle to the church in Rome.

36 This statistic comes from looking personally at 60 different English translations and noting that 32 of them used

'servant' instead of 'deacon'.

37   1 Corinthians 3:5

38   Acts 6:5

39   *Thayer's Greek-English Lexicon* says that 'prostatis' refers to *a woman set over others* and that it describes Phoebe as a *guardian, protector* and *benefactor*. In a more moderate rendering, *Vine's Expository Dictionary of New Testament Words* says that 'prostatis' is a word of *dignity*.

40   In *Life and Times of All the Women of the Bible*, Herbert Lockyer says that *benefactor* in Greek is 'prostatis'. Bob Gass in *The Word for Today* says that this same word was often applied to Olympic coaches who supported athletes and made sure they were trained and equipped to give their best.

41   Herbert Lockyer, *The Life and Times of All the Women of the Bible*, Zondervan 2016. Eddie Hyatt adds in *Charisma Magazine*: 'Some will argue that Phoebe was merely a patroness to Paul who supplied financial support for his ministry. However, the overall sense of the passage, including Paul's designation of her as a "minister," militates against such an interpretation. She was one who had "stood before" others, including Paul himself. An argument could be made from this passage that Phoebe had, at some time, functioned in a pastoral type role toward Paul. She had "stood before" him. She is obviously held in very high esteem by him for he exhorts the Roman believers, both men and women, to receive her and respect her in the Lord in a manner worthy of the saints, and to assist her in whatever business she has need of you. (Romans 16:2)'

www.charismamag.com/spirit/bible-study/32387-meet-the-mighty-women-of-god-who-mentored-paul (accessed 25 October 2019)

42 The term 'coach' came from the practices of early 19th century trainers. Knowing that young men, in the days before phones and social media, could not get themselves to the river early for rowing practice, they would pull up to the boarding house and whistle and hustle the students into the horse-drawn coach and off to training. That is where we first encounter the term 'coach' when used of a trainer.

43 Bob and Debby Gass, *The Word for Today*, 24 June 2019 (Australian version). From *The Word for Today*, published by *Vision Christian Media*. Free introductory issues of this devotional may be obtained (within Australia) from *Vision Christian Media* by phoning 1800 00 777 0

44 www.iep.utm.edu/cynics/ (accessed 2 November 2019)

45 dictionary.cambridge.org/dictionary/english/cynical (accessed 2 November 2019)

46 The five women at the beginning of Exodus are the midwives, Shiphrah and Puah; Miriam, the sister of Moses, and Jochebed, his mother; as well as the unnamed daughter of Pharaoh. The five women at the end of Numbers are Zelophehad's daughters—Mahlah, Tirzah, Hoglah, Milkah and Noah. This curious naming feature is both paralleled and contrasted in Mark's gospel which, after mentioning John the Baptist, begins with the names of four male disciples (Peter, Andrew, James and John) and ends with the names of four female disciples (Mary Magdalene; Mary, the mother of Joses; Mary, the mother of James; and Salome).

More Precious than Pearls

The Mother's Blessing and God's Favour towards Women

Did you know the women of Israel refused to participate in building the golden calf? Or that they were the first to sacrifice their jewellery for the building of the tabernacle?

More Precious than Pearls looks at nuances in the Hebrew text not normally found in English translations. Be surprised by God's joy and His rewards for women—because they so often were steadfast and faithful when the men wavered.

Two versions of this book are available: one with simple study prompts for small groups and one without this study guide. Each version includes prayers for you or for the women in your life. In addition, for mothers or grandmothers, there are special blessings to declare over your children.

ISBN: 978-1-925380-06-4
ISBN: 978-1-925380-22-4 *(Study Guide)*

A French edition, *Plus précieuse que des perles: La bénédiction d'une mère et la faveur de Dieu envers les femmes*, is also available.

www.ingramcontent.com/pod-product-compliance
Lightning Source LLC
Chambersburg PA
CBHW071522080526
44588CB00011B/1532